Memories of
Unsoiled Decay

Memories of Unsoiled Decay

A Masters in Fine Arts Graduate Thesis

Matthew B. Harrison, Esq.

MFA Degree Candidate, Photographer

Emily Therese Louise Jones

Model/Subject, Assistant Editor

Laini Wolman

Associate Editor

KIWI PRESS

NEW YORK

to the extended crew of the
flying harrison brothers:
michael, bernadette,
emily & phoebe

without your support and inspiration

my world would be quite empty

my deepest thanks

additional acknowledgements:
david arnold, dennis cole, will mosgrove
keith sikes, chris weeks, laini wolman

& duncan at foto henny hoogeveen

CONTENTS

The portfolio of images referenced
throughout this book is available online
@ www.memoriesofunsoileddecay.com

INTRODUCTION
By Emily Therese Louise Jones

My experience urban exploring with Matthew began about a year before either of us knew of the Boyce Thompson Institute in Yonkers, NY. Having never visited an abandoned place before, I was intrigued by his proposition to explore and agreed to accompany him to *the School for the Feeble Minded*" in Belchertown, MA. There, following him through a hidden basement window and eventually up to a crumbling yet profoundly beautiful auditorium, I acquired an appreciation for that which had been forgotten and the belief that we must attempt to preserve the past however we can.

The logical means to accomplish this is through memory, our natural mechanism for holding onto what we once had. By documenting our experiences and explorations through the photographic medium, it was possible to preserve what we had seen and touched not only for ourselves, but also for posterity. Memories, at least how I have known them, tend to be inconsistent and of a transient nature. What I mean by this is that they have a tendency to change over time, to preserve only certain elements of an experience while losing details that we cannot readily revisit, and to have different meanings to us in different contexts. In any particular moment it is very easy to take details for granted, like the temperature of the room, or how many books are on the coffee table in our peripheral vision. These things can be in plain sight but not in our focus. The more time passes before we revisit a moment may affect our memory of the experience differently. What my memory of a day at the fair consists of could easily focus not on which rides I stood in line for, but rather on just how good it felt to have the breeze in my hair at the top of the ferris wheel or the smell of fried dough wafting from a nearby concession stand. My literal experience that day might have been dominated by impatience and irritation, but my memory of it later is likely to be limited, subjective, and different in tone when compared to my sentiments at the time the events occurred.

These images, to me, are better than memories. Memories are generally incidental phenomena. We live our lives and when we care to think about our past, we have some vague thought about the things that have happened to us. These images are deliberate moments. We went to the greenhouse for the purpose of exploring and documenting the location, but also to document what happened when we went there. We chose clothing reminiscent of vintage styling because that which appeared to be from the past struck me as being most effective at conveying that the images were of the past and not captures of a current reality. I chose to emote in a ways reflective of how both Matthew and I felt about the space at those moments. Matthew chose to use the equipment that he did for their practical and aesthetic qualities, to document what happened the way he wanted to see it. There is no objectivity in this approach. The fact that much of the process was deliberate is so appropriate for the concept of creating memories because memories are inherently subjective and are whatever we make of them. At the same time, elements of chance were present in our equation as they are in the natural development of memories. Our experiences and the photos were affected by various circumstances beyond our control, such as the weather, changing states of daylight, the growth and death of wild vegetation surrounding the greenhouse, and the occasional company of a resident cat. So our memories and the photographs are not entirely manufactured, but rather molded by what parts of our circumstances we realistically had the power to affect. Likewise, we can control our experiences in life to a certain extent and therefore can affect our memories of our lives, but the memories are malleable and subject to the whims of both time and our subconscious.

Looking back on the images from the many trips we made to the greenhouse in Yonkers, I see a girl who looks very much like me experiencing wonder, curiosity, dismay, fear, and hope in what could easily be mistaken for a barren loss of what was once a place of progress. I glean insight from her expression, from the colors of the image and how cold the snow looks. Having personally been there in those moments, the images trigger literal memories of what happened there. I remember the berries of the bittersweet cascading down through the broken glass roof, and of searching for my hat that I had set down somewhere. The images, on another level, allow me to see these same moments as Matthew saw them. I see myself as he saw me, and how he saw the greenhouse, with all of its fascinating lines and geometry that I had failed to appreciate when immersed in its architecture. So by layering these perspectives of the same moments, I feel much closer to a sort of truth. I feel more connected to him, being able to experience moments I shared with him in the way that he did and focus on the elements he saw most worthy of preservation. While the images have literal meaning for me, they are intended to touch the arbitrary viewer as well. Perhaps the broken glass will conjure someone's childhood memory, or the sight of snow coupled with my lightweight dress might send chills down a viewer's spine.

What is important is that different people are able to relate to the images on individual and personal levels, thereby providing a new perspective on a personal moment. This act of relating and sharing perspectives is the key to achieving a greater understanding of truth than we can know if confined to our own experience of the world.

PREFACE

"Many pictures turn out to be limp translations of the known world instead of vital objects which create an intrinsic world of their own. There is a vast difference between taking a picture and making a photograph." - Robert Heinecken

Many people take snapshots. They use a camera to document the eye catching visuals of a moment, encapsulating it for posterity. Their primary objective is to convey a **literal truth**[1] to the viewer/recipient by means of a photograph. The viewers are receptive to this literal truth, as inherent to the snapshot viewing process is the suspension of disbelief that allows a snapshot's content to be perceived as truth represented in photographic form.

In most cases, the viewer has a direct connection to the content of the image; they were one of the participants – or have an interest in the subject matter. When the photograph is supported by personal memory, it is hard to identify how the photographic process may have manipulated the actual truth of the original scene. [2]

The mark of an artist is the realization that a camera is not some type of mechanical doppelganger to the eye. A camera sees differently than our eyes do and can be used as a means to communicate a story. For most artists – the story goes beyond themselves and capturing moments from their lives and the literal content contained within the frame. The photographs no longer reveal literal truth but instead present a metaphor for a **greater truth**.[3,4] The viewer is engaged in identifying

---

[1]   **Literal truth**, as used throughout this paper, specifically refers to the actual content contained within the frame of a photograph. No weight is given to formalism.

[2]   I purport my photographs only to be photographs. While there are aspects of reality depicted – it is still just a moment in time recorded and manipulated by me personally using numerous inanimate objects.

[3]   **Greater truth**, as used throughout this paper, specifically refers to a photograph as the product of the content itself and the form in which that content is presented.

[4]   There are many examples of this metaphor in modern photography. One example is the work of Robert and Shana Parke-Harrison. While their work is literally a series of self portraits, they are

the metaphor and appreciating the relationship that the photographer has demonstrated with the subject.

This portfolio contains both categories as components of the larger work. The content has literal meaning to those involved or interested in the subject matter, and the portfolio is a metaphor for my own emotional growth during the almost two year long process. However, there is a third component of this portfolio that makes it worthy of being the work product of a Masters Degree Scholar: these photographs were specifically created in such a way as to maximize a viewers engagement with these images. I applied scientific research to my photographic process – in order to maximize the portfolio's ability to engage the viewer.

The purpose of this methodology was to trigger memories in the minds of the viewers – as if they were directly involved with the particular image – therefore allowing the viewer to relate to both the artist and the subject individually, and the relationship they have with each other in the image.[5]

---

larger metaphors for humanities effect on nature, whether it is marks we leave on the earth, or the destruction of entire landscapes for materialistic purposes

[5] An alternative title for this portfolio could be *What is the meaning of life?* As this is my answer – or at least my attempt to identify an objective truth. The question inherently seeks objectivity, i.e. an answer that is universal to all people at all times and space; yet any attempt to respond is supported by one's own personal experience – thereby exposing this truth to personal bias – thereby removing its objectivity.

ABSTRACT

An artist realizes that the view from a camera and the eyes are not the same. By controlling the camera and how it sees, one controls a viewer's connection with a particular work.

These fine art photographs were taken over a year of explorations at an abandoned greenhouse in Yonkers, New York. They depict the literal explorations and discoveries of Emily Therese, and her documentation and re-appropriation of the resources of this abandonment. They also serve as the culmination of my own emotional re-appropriation of resources and the discovery of the beauty within the decay that was a significant part of my own circumstances.

I created these images to maximize the viewer's engagement with the photographs, in an attempt to increase their relationship with the photograph, and the relationship between the photographer and the subject.

I made specific decisions about my content and its capture, including format and equipment. These choices resulted from the application of extensive scientific research on vision and perception to my photographic process.

This portfolio contains 18 images output onto 12" x 18" sheets of brushed aluminum. They have been treated using an adapted dye sublimation process and coated so as to be glossy - you can see yourself in them.

I. THE PARADOX OF PHOTOGRAPHY

Artists often seek objective truth by means of their particular medium. While there may not be a universally accepted articulation of objectivity, a proposition is generally considered to be objectively true when it is not the result of any judgments made by a conscious entity.

Scientific knowledge is systematic knowledge of the nature of existing things, as we perceive them, as opposed to how things are in actuality. This seems to be the accepted train of thought since Critique of Pure Reason by Immanuel Kant.

Photography, as a process to capture authenticity and truth, has been examined exhaustively.[6] It can be concluded that any proffer of truth is tainted by means of the artist's subjectivity.[7] The composition of a particular scene, the equipment used, and the locations selected, or even the determination of the decisive moment, are all manifestations of personal bias.

Objectivity does not exist in Science because all scientific methods and measurements are based on human tools and ideas (i.e. bias) though we are in search of objective truths about the natural world within our own subjective means.

In Art, the objective truth is not prized as much as the relevance of an artist's subjective truth to others as well as to himself. [8]

An artist creates for his or her own personal reasons, but by showing a particular work an artist is attempting to harmonize their subjective truth with the subjective truth of the viewer, thereby enabling the viewer to gain better perspective of a larger truth. Because the viewer

---

[6]   Snapshots offered as truth are assumed to have captured a scene as close as possible to the human condition. See *preface.*

[7]   This is the paradox – for purposes of this paper.

[8]   While we can never truly see objectively, we can approximate it by increasing our experiences and gaining as much perspective as possible to make an accurate or educated guess.

can only relate his or her interpretation of the artist's work with his or her own experiences, it is necessary for the artist to offer their truth by means of the message and its presentation.[9]

By comparing his or her own subjective truth based upon personal experience, with the subjective truth that the artist is presenting, the viewer gains perspective. It would seem that the only way to achieve true objectivity then, would be through exposure to the entire variety of bias. Because we can only experience so much in our lives, our understanding is only partially complete. Therefore subjectivity is the only truth in which one can operate.

A. I SHOOT THEREFORE I AM (BIAS)

Cognition proves existence.[10] Nevertheless, our thoughts do not exist alone inside a vacuum; rather they are the natural reactions to stimuli experienced by our bodies.[11] Despite our certainty of the concrete nature of our reality – our senses are not perfect. Additionally, some matters cannot even be measured with our senses and are subject to notational bias inherent with the use of instrumentation. Furthermore, a viewer's cultural history can also cloud their perspective.

---

[9]   Form versus content. What the message says versus how the message is said. This includes all of the visual elements featured within the frame, but also how they are presented including the medium.

[10]   Descartes' original statement was "Je pense donc je suis," from his Discourse on Method (1637). He wrote it in French, not in Latin, intending to reach a wider audience in his country than that of scholars. He uses the Latin "Cogito ergo sum" in the later Principles of Philosophy (1644), Part 1, article 7: "Ac proinde hæc cognitio, ego cogito, ergo sum, est omnium prima & certissima, quæ cuilibet ordine philosophanti occurrat.".

[11]   These stimuli must start as physical, but substantial scientific documentation states that the memory can replay the stimulus (both consciously and unconsciously), activating the same brain chemistry as if it were actually happening physically.

Since our memories are based upon these stimulations[12] that had been experienced by our senses, which we have already established are inherently subjective – then our thoughts and memories must also be subjective.

This subjectivity applies to my photography. These photographs are my subjective truth. I went to those places and took those photographs. But the photographs, and the reality depicted within, have been purposefully manipulated. I did this to create a metaphor for changes in my own life: a re-appropriation of elements from within the emptiness and decay of my existence. This manipulation was also done in such a way as to maximize a viewer's ability to relate to the particular photograph by having it stimulate their memories and experiences.

I have come to the conclusion that a viewer's reaction to a particular work depends upon his or her own previous experience and personal bias. If the bias of the viewer and the bias of the artist are the same a relationship forms over the work.[13] When, however, the bias of the viewer and the bias of the artist are different – yet the work touches both similarly – the relationship is strongest and the work becomes much more effective at engaging the viewer.[14]

1. THE LINK BETWEEN PHOTOGRAPHS AND MEMORY

For many people, details and specifics become hazy as time passes. This happens because the mind is incapable of maintaining exact information for long periods of time without proper reinforcement. Otherwise generalized feelings and emotion are all that remain to summarize the experience.

---

[12] I explore the science behind this later in the paper.

[13] For the purpose of making a comparison, if this were a bond between atoms it would be referred to as ionic bonding. It is the second weakest bond. The weakest bond is hydrogen bonding and would correspond to the snapshot, which was defined previously.

[14] The chemical equivalent would be the covalent bonds, which are the strongest bonds, and for my purposes, the most desirable.

Moments are often deemed unimportant and forgotten unless the brain determines that they have a specific purpose. This usually occurs when the sensory cells are super-stimulated, especially when sensations include multiple sensory elements such as both smell and taste. These sensory elements are two often-cited triggers of memories.[15] Of course these two sensations are not an exhaustive list.

A photograph reinforces memories by providing constant and repeated stimulation allowing the mind to adequately record a response. When experiences happen in real time, the brain is flooded with stimulation and it often requires a significant amount thereof for something in particular to permeate the consciousness. By viewing a photograph over an extended period of time, one is able to focus on multiple visual elements and make the necessary connections in order to gain any sort of lasting understanding.[16]

Perhaps this is the underlying purpose of the snapshot: to provide the necessary stimulation to trigger the memories associated with the scene in the particular photograph[17]. The association does not need to be logical, as the mind frequently creates abstract connections as are made in memories.[18]

---

[15] Think about examples in your own life when you smell something in particular and your mind is instantly transported to a time when you experienced a similar sensation. There is even an urban legend that suggests baking apple pies or cookies while a home for sale is being shown will make that home more appealing to prospective purchasers. The hope is that the brain's positive association with that smell will be associated additionally with the house.

[16] My editor suggests that I need a citation for this particular statement. I disagree, as I believe that this is a restatement of common knowledge, just expressed in a particular manner as to relate to my thesis.

[17] This is not to be confused with the snapshot aesthetic. I am specifically referring to the type of photographs kept in scrapbooks and yearbooks. Their sole purpose for existing is to remind the viewer of their own memories as triggered by the photograph. The association is personal.

[18] Associating a particular circumstance with a particular song is similar.

A snapshot is the perfect medium when the purpose of creating an image is to trigger memories contained within the mind of the photographer.[19] Ideally, it is the photographer who would know how to best capture or convey the content of an image to maximize its ability to trigger a personal association.

When I examine the photographs presented in this portfolio, particular details emerge as meaningful enough to merit their capture in a photograph. It is by viewing them over an extended period of time that my mind begins to identify the context and gains clarity that would otherwise be impossible to obtain in real time.[20]

Before suspension of disbelief begins, it is necessary to understand that these photographs are in no way accurate representations of that which was seen by my eyes and processed by my mind, despite the fact that human nature is to perceive photographs as being accurate representations of an objective truth. I can only offer these images to act as a representation of the things that I deemed important enough to want to remember.

So not only is the content focused on things I deemed important enough to want to remember, but these photographs were constructed in such a manner as to trigger these memories more effectively than a typical snapshot would. Considering that these images were created for an audience larger than myself, and for a purpose greater than to remind me of my adventures, the application of the science of perception to my image making process allows the viewer to relate to the image as if they had a personal connection to the moment captured.[21]

---

[19]   Or other participants present at the creation of the photograph.

[20]   Photography is a commonly used method of documentation, becoming increasingly more acceptable for the self and for others with the proliferation of inexpensive and unobtrusive digital technology. Even Leica makes at least three different lines of point and shoot cameras – though none of them were used in the making of this portfolio.

[21]   This is the essence of my thesis. In case there was any doubt.

These photographs are manifestations of the way I choose to remember my experiences at the abandoned greenhouse. Together as a portfolio, the photographs present not only the literal story of Emily Therese, but also a personal metaphor about finding beauty within decay. The images should also trigger memories in the mind of the viewer in order for them to make a comparison of my subjective truth with their own.

The image does not throw itself on the viewer to cement this relationship by means of its content[22]; instead the elements of the image super stimulate the sensory cells of the viewer in such a manner as to trigger emotions or memories that their brain as already pre-determined to be relevant (by means of location within the neural network[23]). The ability for me, as photographer, to create images that engage the viewer to relate to the portfolio is what makes these images unique.

So while you may not understand my true feelings that day, the smell of the greenhouse, my apprehension due to tighter security at the location, or any one of a million personal truths related to the picture-taking experience, it really does not matter. What is important is that your brain conjures up your own personal truth; based upon your own personal experiences, allowing your mind to make a seamless comparison in a language it truly understands.

The resulting mental images evoked in the viewers mind are what I call **indirect memories.**[24] The photographs in this portfolio were designed

---

[22]   This body of work is not shocking. On it's face, they may look like storybook illustrations; almost lulling the viewer into a sense of security. Unlike those images where there's a gun to someone's head and it's milliseconds before the trigger is pulled.

[23]   A neural network is a group of neurons that are interconnected. Arbib, Michael A. (Ed.) (2003). The Handbook of Brain Theory and Neural Networks.

[24]   These are not memories or emotions that were actually depicted in the image – but develop upon comparison with one's own experience. So while a photograph can stimulate the sensory cells to trigger an original memory (in the mind of a participant), it can also be used to trigger memories of a similar nature (in the minds of those with no literal connection) based upon their location within the nearby neural net.

to maximize the trigger of any potential associations or indirect memories.

This intention to trigger memories becomes a useful tool when an artist is capturing and creating literal content of an image to be used as a metaphor for a larger message. A view of such photos detects three different perspectives: the literal content of the photograph, the artist's intended metaphor, and the viewer's metaphor that emerges from comparing the reality of what is depicted with what is experienced internally.

Memories of Unsoiled Decay: Thesis Portfolio explores the abandoned greenhouse in Yonkers, New York. I have created a body of work meant to convey a metaphor communicating my subjective truth that triggers a viewer's memory of their own experiences. This creates their own point of comparison, and comparing them both results in the identification and connection to the intended metaphor.

2. THE MIND AS CAMERA

Consciousness – at its core – is our individualized, self-controlled response to external stimulation. There exist a few examples of self-controlled responses to external stimulation that are not conscious – such as increase adrenaline during frightening circumstances – but these are not the responses to which I am referring. Humanity is driven toward furthering its exposure to external stimulation, as the mind would die without such. [25] But our biology is not perfect, and while our brains may process this consciousness – it doesn't know the final destination for any of the "data." It does not know what becomes a stored memory, nor does it necessarily know how to retrieve previously stored information accurately.

---

[25]   Again, my editor suggests that a footnote is necessary for this particular conclusion. I disagree, as I believe that I am simply articulating common knowledge that humans need physical and mental sustenance in order to survive.

It is impossible to create an accurate representation of reality, because it is impossible to divorce the subject perceived from the person doing the perceiving, regardless of method of capture. The human brain simply lacks the capacity to do so.[26] If the brain were capable of perceiving an accurate reflection of reality, our minds would immediately reject it.[2728] This would result in an existential crisis. Our mind protects itself by suspending disbelief so as not to allow such a crisis to occur.[29]

As a result of this inherent suspension of disbelief, it is only necessary for a particular work to focus on a limited number of aspects of reality in order to maintain believability. The human mind can only process and render certain aspects of the experienced stimulation. By streamlining the processes at capture to only focus on these certain aspects, the image will be viewed in such a way as to optimize the image's potential for stimulation of the viewer.

To maximize the stimulation factor of a photograph, it must contain not only the memory-triggering literal content but also a harmonious

---

[26]   Matthew B. Harrison, This Paper.

[27]   As never having experienced reality without bias, an unbiased reality would not be believable, as human understanding relies upon subjective comparisons. Again – the root of the paradox – and without balance, there can only exist crisis and tension.

[28]   "Life is a train of moods like a string of beads; and as we pass through them they prove to be many colored lenses, which paint the world their own hue, and each shows us only what lies in its own focus." Ralph Waldo Emerson.

[29]   One of the flaws with increased digital technology is that movies and photographs are becoming endless canvases for details. While our eyes cannot notice every detail of every second seen within our lifetime – we are able to focus on such details within the limited universe of a photograph or a movie. As the detail increases – by means of resolution and digital artistry – the audience's suspension of disbelief must increase concurrently.

presentation of that content in a manner that furthers its underlying message.

One of the masterful demonstrations of this relationship between form and content is in the ability to identify and photograph examples of visual tension, either within the content of the image or in the way the content of the image is presented.

Memories of Unsoiled Decay is an ironic exploration into this visual tension, as there are many examples of such irony inherent to the exploration of abandoned buildings. The buildings may appear dark and dangerous but they are sources for much elegance within the decay.

B. THE DIRECT MEMORY

I enjoy exploring abandoned buildings: specifically those that have long been abandoned and untouched, especially those with the original contents still inside.

It started in late October 2006, when I first adventured to The School for the Feeble Minded in Belchertown, Massachusetts. I went with another photographer[30] and three models.[31] I was hooked from the moment we entered into the dark abyss that was one of the remaining patient houses. Our flashlights lit a long-forgotten past unseen for more than 20 years.

With my background in cinema and theater, these places seemed like perfect locations in which to act out an improvisational play that would be captured by my photographic lens.

The locations may have been abandoned but they were certainly far from empty. Every inch of space was covered in something – whether it was dust from the decomposition, vintage books, patient files, personal belongings, or even industrial green paint. Each room within

---

[30] Long time friend and shooting partner, Lesley Arak.

[31] Sara Patterson, Amelia Houghton, and Cassandra Mulcahy.

each building was a separate universe in which to act out many different realities.

This location was one of 16 state medical facilities in Massachusetts. There were many more within New England. I have also visited abandoned factories, police stations, community colleges, and of course, the abandoned greenhouse in Yonkers, New York.

This portfolio of photographs factually consists of model-based explorations at an abandoned greenhouse in Yonkers, New York. These photographs are not memories themselves, as they are just plates of brushed aluminum that have been treated by means of a dye sublimation process in order to display the desired image in the desired manner. However, the literal meaning prescribed by these representations is not open to interpretation.

The explorations were real. They took place over the course of a calendar year. The images feature a model wearing a yellow dress.[32] The photographs, though they seem as if they were taken directly from the camera, are actually composites, having multiple layers from multiple exposures present. All of the digital components used in the making of these photographs were taken during these explorations. The base images were created from digital and film images that captured our actual moments in time and space.

A viewer can understand these as snapshots provided that they are aware that the model is an actual person, the greenhouse is an actual place, and these photos are of actual explorations.

1. MY SNAPSHOT IN TIME

It begins with flowers. Eighteenth-century scientist John Dalton was a professor of Mathematics and Natural Philosophy at New College, Manchester, England. In the early 1790s, he became aware that his

---

[32]   Emily Therese, my then-girlfriend and now fiancée.

vision differed from others when he could not accurately discern between blue and pink flowers.[33]

I found this particularly meaningful, as that the study of photography led me to discover that I suffer from a unique genetic form of color blindness that makes it difficult for me to differentiate between certain shades of blue and certain shades of yellow.

This made the abandoned greenhouse and school for botanical study the perfect location for my thesis project. Most of my previous locations were abandoned psychiatric facilities. But unlike most urban explorers, I had no ties to those locations; my interest was purely aesthetic.[34] However, this abandoned greenhouse was different than any of my previous exploration sites – as the connection to the location became very personal.

It seems as if both Dalton and I discovered our own physical limitations by exercising our passions. The abandoned greenhouse in Yonkers, NY has allowed me to combine both of our passions and draw conclusions shedding new light upon the age old question: how accurately do I see the world?

2. THE LOCATION

The abandoned greenhouse in Yonkers, NY is called the Boyce Thompson Institute for Plant Research. The idea for the facility came in 1917, when William Boyce Thompson took part in a Red Cross "relief" mission sent by President Woodrow Wilson to prevent Russia from

---

[33] Vision and Art: The Biology of Seeing, Margaret Livingstone. Pp. 33.

[34] Though certainly not verifiable as a usable statistic concerning the body of urban explorers, there exist many first-hand accounts of personal experiences at the various locations as being the desire to go back and explore again. While there are no formal sources, such illustrative conversations resulting in those conclusions are not citable.

entering World War I and to encourage the formation of a democratic government there.

Thompson witnessed much suffering and starvation as the result of the socialist government's inability to take care of its own people. Upon return from his experience in Russia, Thompson was convinced "that agriculture, food supply, and social justice are linked. World political stability in the future," he prophesied, "would depend on the availability of adequate food." This conviction, along with his faith in science, helped to shape his next philanthropic project.[35]

And so in 1919, he began to obtain property to house the Boyce Thompson Institute for Plant Research opposite his Yonkers home. It was created with an initial investment of $1 million dollars, an amount to which much more was added over the years.

The Institute was formally dedicated on September 24, 1924. The original building had a total floor space of 85,764 sq. ft. There was an arboretum and greenhouse space of over 16,000 sq. ft. The Institute also used to own more than 300 acres of rich agricultural land for field plots, though this has since been sold and developed.

The Boyce Thompson Institute continued important research and innovation at its Yonkers location for more than 50 years. The pollution of the Hudson River spawned extensive research into the subject, and in 1977 the Institute, under the project leadership of Edward H. Buckley, published *An Atlas of the Biologic Resources of the Hudson Estuary*. Just over a year later, however, the Institute moved to Cornell University in Ithaca, New York, as cooperation with the educational institution offered advantages into research opportunities and the Institute could not/did not want to pay the higher property taxes of an increasingly urbanized locale. The Boyce Thompson Institute today operates as an independent organization in cooperation with Cornell University, while the shell of the once building and greenhouse remain lost in Yonkers.

---

[35]   History Overview; Boyce Thompson Institute for Plant Research. Web. Jan. 2010.

3. THE PLAN

Empty land became a working science center for 54 years until one day it lay abandoned. Thirty-six years later I stumbled onto the grounds and began to re-appropriate the original elements to create these photographs. This theme of re-appropriation is inherent to urban exploration, and it reverberates throughout the location and my thesis.

I do not go exploring alone. Nor do I take photographs of just the abandoned locations.[36] I bring a model. In this case, I brought my fiancée Emily Therese.

The plan was to make numerous trips to the location at all hours of the night and day; throughout a variety of seasons and weather events; over the course of an entire year; and to document our discoveries at the greenhouse.

This plan was executed successfully without incident or arrest. There were over 800 exposures taken during the numerous trips to the abandonment. Sixty images have been edited. Twenty are included in this particular portfolio.

---

[36]   Neither Matthew B. Harrison nor any of his affiliates can be held liable for your arrest, injury, or death while exploring. You are responsible for your own actions. If you decide to explore, please remember that many abandoned places are private property, and are patrolled by police, private security firms, or the owners themselves. You may be ticketed, arrested or even shot at while trespassing on these grounds. Since the buildings are not maintained, it is possible to become afflicted with health problems related to asbestos, lead, tetanus, bird droppings, and mold exposure.

4. THE SNAPSHOTS

Looking at these photographs, there are two very basic levels of understanding within the entire portfolio.

On the primary level these photographs document the adventures of Emily Therese as she explores the abandoned greenhouse. They show how Emily's actions and emotions evolve from curiosity and wonder to exploration and discovery of this forgotten place.

On the secondary level is the visual irony. There are plants growing wild in a building that formally favored controlled environments. Emily Therese is not a scientist, as those who worked at Boyce Thompson, but instead is a model in a fine art work. Her documentation seems to be of nothing, though this is not the case as the contents of the photographs are far from empty.

There is certainly greater meaning prescribed to these purposeful decisions, but this section is merely about identifying the important literal elements of the images. For these are the elements I chose to remember when making these photographs.

The original intent was for Emily's outfit to remain the same throughout the explorations. We had not yet experienced winter in Yonkers, New York, however. Due to the cold we had no choice but to add a coat and a hat to the original outfit.

The dress is vintage inspired, re-appropriating old trends into a modern dress that just so happens to be the exact color frequency needed for the trigger portion of this paper. The boots were one of Emily's favorite pairs. Her fashions are often featured in my work.

The coat is truly a unique item. Emily's mother made the coat from fabric purchased by her grandmother for use in another project, and was forgotten until long after her passing. While the coat itself may not be vintage, its re-appropriation spans three generations.

5. SNAPSHOTS ARE NOT THE COMPLETE PICTURE

All of the images contained in this portfolio[37] consist of components I felt were important to remember. The importance is conveyed to the viewer initially by the fact that the photograph even exists, and it is reinforced when the events portrayed are remembered or related to something similar in their own minds. The literal elements contained within the frame, though extremely important, are only the first dimension of these photographs.

II. THE METAPHOR

There may be actual truth in the photographic capture process and consequently contained within the boundaries of a snapshot. Nonetheless, the inherent limitations on the ability of the photographic medium to capture objective truth are so numerous that most artists avoid the snapshot altogether.

Instead of ignoring these limitations, I chose to manipulate them in order to convey particular meaning. These photographs are really manifestations of the relationship between the photographer and the subject matter, both the contents and their arrangement. In this case, the images are a metaphor for my emotional relationship with myself.

I am best able to communicate complicated emotional concepts through the creation of visual metaphors.[38] It must be acknowledged that this is a subjective process. The human mind is not capable of an "objective" view, as both the artist and the viewer are encapsulated by their own

---

[37]   While the portfolio, as presented, will include between 16 and 20 images, the entire body of work consists of in excess of 60 images. Furthermore, some images contain elements from other images. Therefore, the total number of images contained is larger than it seems.

[38]   Personal bias in the form of language and culture is a primary justification.

18

experiences. Furthermore I have introduced bias into the interpretation of these photos with deliberate choices of specific stimuli. Identifying the choices to be made is the first step towards communicating the greater metaphor.

First, I used a female protagonist instead of myself, for two major reasons. One: the stereotype that females are widely associated with being more in touch with their emotions than their male counterparts would trigger a readiness and perhaps expectation of emotional content.[39] Two: I have few photos of myself engaged in activities unrelated to my role as photographer. I consider it to be a common curse that afflicts most photographers. It may seem silly, but breaking with tradition solely for the purposes of my thesis was not possible.

The second deliberate choice was the location. My creation of photographs for this project did not start with the abandoned greenhouse. Instead it began in an abandoned medical facility.

I was seemingly obsessed with medicine. My mother was very ill, and since age five I spent significant amounts of time in the waiting rooms of hospitals across New England. The difference between these hospitals and the abandoned ones I visited on photographic explorations was their relation to time; one was an active facility while the other was abandoned. However, there are similar elements of beauty present in both.

After thoroughly researching each location and its abandonment, it became apparent that I needed to expand beyond medical facilities. The feelings (of life outside photography) I associated with them clouded the beauty and the aesthetic of my work. This is why I chose the greenhouse, in addition to homage to Dalton, with whom I share the

---

[39]   I am not suggesting this stereotype is true – nor am I offering it as truth – instead, I suggest that it is this bias that will help further one's relation with the metaphor; which is the purpose of the metaphor.

self-discovery of colorblindness through the pursuit of our life dreams.[40]

This body of work is the result of efforts to conquer my disabilities. As I began to explore and understand the disability, I altered my methods of image construction. I strove to create ideal visual elements to act as triggers for a viewer; whether that viewer was myself or someone else. It is ironic that these ideal visual elements can only be fully appreciated by those without the disability.

At midpoint my work was about abandonment as a place of forgotten ruin and somewhere within the waste was some sort of beauty. Like many before me, I was searching for beauty within the entropy. However upon completion of this body of work, I believe that the true beauty was actually the antithesis of entropy, but rather re-growth and re-appropriation of wasted resources. Indeed, it is the natural tendency of the universe to move towards order and away from entropy.

This was a lesson with a great deal of personal meaning for me. Sadly, my mother succumbed to her extended illness in late 2006. I dwelled upon the loss of my mother in an attempt to find meaning, yet I only got lost in the decay. Being lost in one's own thoughts results in entropy within one's own physical surroundings. It was not until I re-appropriated my own resources that I was able to find new beauty growing around me.

The photos in the portfolio show Emily in the greenhouse, exploring and discovering that nature conquers entropy. But they also present my own discovery that there can be growth from within tremendous destruction.

---

[40]   The change in location mirrored a change in my own life as both emerged from the hopeless world of the rubble of abandoned medical facilities, re-appropriating my emotions into new locations resulting in a different flavor of work. A work based in hope. With the change in location also came a change in equipment.

A. THE AESTHETIC OF MEMORY

My mother always used to tell me in college and in law school that if I attended class, I wouldn't have a problem on exams, as my memory would soak up the important things just from experiencing them.

I am a very visual person. Most of my memories center on a visual, whether it's the knick-knacks on my grandmother's coffee table, or the way Emily Therese's hair moved in the wind in the pre-sunrise hours at some of our photo shoots. There was much truth in my mother's words; my memory requires visual stimulation in order to be effective.

I think the concept of photographic memory – as I have been described as having – is nothing more than an oxymoronic misnomer. Memory is anything but photographic – even for visual oriented people, such as myself.

As I mentioned previously, and will continue to detail in the remaining sections of this paper, memory is inherently hazy. Unless we spend conscious effort to remember something, it is left to our subconscious to determine what is important enough stimulation worthy of either short or long term storage.

Individual memories tend to only focus on one particular item, idea, or concept: the name of your lab partner in 7th grade science class; the smell of the little league field after it was freshly mowed; the voice of a deceased parent imparting lifelong words of wisdom.

Could you describe your lab partners face to a sketch artist? Could you name any of the advertisers listed on the billboards surrounding the field? What about what they were wearing when they imparted that knowledge? If these questions can be answered, it's more than likely due to the fact that the answer would be considered personally important. Otherwise, such excess details are removed and forgotten.

Mastery of a shallow depth of field is a vital component to reproducing an aesthetic similar to a memory. By having the ability to select the focus with the amount of precision afforded by the 50mm/0.95

Noctilux, the photographer can focus the attention of the viewer, guiding them towards the important aspects by maintaining a shallow focus on only those parts.

Additionally, each photograph is actual composited with layers featuring whole or sections of additional images taken at the abandoned greenhouse. By layering these visuals together, I was able to stimulate the viewer into making particular associations, in order to gain an overall sense of a particular scene. This composite is not true to reality, but much more similar to actual memory – as often times components of our memories contain associations created from other memories or experiences.

Specifically, a few of the images feature specular highlights deliberately captured out of focus in order to add the whimsical feelings inherent to visuals of such bokeh blurring.

B. THERE IS A SEASON, TURN, TURN, TURN

This haziness extends to all aspects of a memory. The photographs have incorporated a number of aspects of how the collected experiences at the abandoned greenhouse have rendered themselves in my mind.

A lot of my selected focus is on Emily Therese's eyes. In part, this was to stimulate the viewer mentally by attempting to recognize the face, but to also key in on what I consider to be the most important part of a person (and ultimately my best tool for identification), one's eyes.

The latest Noctilux affords the shallowest depth of field currently available on the market. There are a few experimental lenses that do have faster apertures, but do not have even remotely close to the level of quality in manufacture, as does the Leica lens.

During the preparations for this thesis portfolio, it was required that I submit some in progress samples in order to gauge the level of completion. I submitted a selected portfolio that evoked the following question: "Were these shot on the same day? There is a lot of similarity here."

This was a conscious choice. There was only one outfit featured throughout the entire portfolio. There were some accessories that have been added in some of the images due to the nature of the weather conditions at the time of shooting. Additionally, the hair, makeup, and daylight conditions varied throughout the thirteen different shooting exercises.

The purpose of keeping things mostly similar – yet varying enough of the external details – was to simulate the aesthetic of memory.

Using myself as an example, I have been a Massachusetts attorney since late 2005. One of the most common associations with an attorney, beyond being the butt of an endless amount of jokes, is that they wear suits. As an arts, entertainment, and media attorney – a large segment of my client base does not wear suits, and would be intimidated by anyone (especially their lawyer) if they wore a suit at a client meeting. That being said, a suit is generally not a part of my regular wardrobe.

Any memory of myself that I have in the capacity as lawyer, has me wearing a suit. If I were to create a photograph of any such memory – I would be sure to include my wearing a suit. Yet, I can only think of a handful of times in the past year that I actually wore a suit – though all of them were related to my being a lawyer.

The point is that our minds play tricks on us. When we don't remember the specific details, our minds fill them in with enough information so as to maintain believability. Obviously, at my core, I believe that being a lawyer requires wearing a suit and as such, I make sure to outfit myself in one for every memory.

The same is true for this portfolio. It was important that Emily Therese be featured in a particular yellow outfit. This detail remained the same – just as my suit remains the same in my own memories.

Additionally, the portfolio features the constructed element of frozen time. Each image featured a high enough shutter speed so as to maintain extreme sharpness in the in-focus areas, as to give the appearance of freezing these moments in time forever. The problem with this frozen moment paradigm is that it appears to have lost any semblance of time passing. The different seasons provide for an ebb and flow of the tide of re-growth in the abandoned greenhouse, which provide the viewer with the reality that these images were not taken on the same day, at the same time, or even during the same season. Some of the images have morning light. Others were taken during mid-day or afternoon lighting conditions. Some of the images feature snow or other inclement weather conditions. Other images feature bright sunshine. Additionally, there is the change in the growth due to the change in the seasons.

III. THE TRIGGER

These photographs were scientifically created in order to trigger memories in the mind of the viewer to maximize their relationship with the work. This section of the paper is broken down into three subsections: A) The science of memory; B) My choices in equipment to execute this project; C) The application of the science to my photo making process.

A. THE SCIENCE OF MEMORY

In theory, humans all process information the same way. This is inherent to our biological makeup as members of the same species with the same general biological processes. We make comparisons based upon our own individualized experiences and sensations.

If human biology determines how to process stimulation received from the sensory cells, then manipulation[41] of this process can change the resulting meanings of the stimulations.

---

[41]   I know that the term manipulation is loaded and contains a negative connotation, but here, manipulation is not necessarily deviously intended, such as when one tries to forget disturbing memories, or

24

In photography it is possible to manipulate the stimuli that the camera records. Therefore, *ceteris paribus,* then adjustment to the image by the photographer will result in manipulation of the type of memory triggered, if any is triggered at all.

On the scientific level, memories are the electrochemical renderings of visual images captured by the eyes, combined with stimulation from our other sensory organs, processed into permanence by the brain during our sleep cycle. If the means through which sensory cells receive the stimulation is altered, so will the electrochemical renderings processed by the brain.

This process is similar to the photographic process. Light bouncing off the subject travels through the glass lens, striking a sensor, thereby creating an electronic rendering of the original visual image, which is turned into a series of binary code to be processed by a computer before becoming permanent during the printing cycle.

By understanding how our bodies receive and process their external stimulation, it is possible to manipulate these stimuli to produce desired results.

1. IT STARTS WITH A NEURON

A neuron is a cell in the nervous system that processes and transmits information by electrical signaling.[42] Our brain consists of hundreds of billions of neurons that connect to tens of thousands of others, forging a

---

remembers one's contribution to the big game as being much more significant than it actually was.

[42]   Davies, Melissa. "Neuroscience - A Journey Through the Brain." University of Alberta.

network of 100 to1000 trillion connections strung together by 90 million meters of neural fibers.[43]

The brain consists of six distinct tissue layers, each with its own set of interconnecting neurons. These neurons communicate with each other through electrical impulses sent from the nucleus of each cell, down axons (transmitter sites) and across to dendrites (receptor sites) of the surrounding neurons.[44] These "links of a chain" allows the brain to communicate with the body it controls.

2. THE ACTION HAPPENS IN THE SYNAPSE

Most of the action takes place in the synapse, a specialized junction through which neurons communicate. A neuron sends a signal to its neighbor by releasing packets of a particular neurotransmitter (most axon terminals release only one specific neurotransmitter), and those are received by specialized receptors at the dendrites of the receiving neuron. [45]

The human brain has an unfathomable number of synapses. Each of the $1x10^{11}$ (one hundred billion) neurons has on average 7,000 synaptic connections to other neurons. [46]A three-year-old child has about $1x10^{15}$ synapses (1 quadrillion). This number declines with age, stabilizing by adulthood. Estimates vary for an adult, ranging from $1x10^{14}$ to $5 x 10^{14}$ synapses (100 to 500 trillion).[47]

---

[43]   "The Brain-addiction Connection : Neurons and Neurotransmitters | All About Addiction."

[44]   Davies, Melissa. "Neuroscience - A Journey Through the Brain." University of Alberta.

[45]   "The Brain-addiction Connection : Neurons and Neurotransmitters | All About Addiction."

[46]   Kandel, Eric R.; James H. Schwartz, Thomas M. Jessell (2000). Principles of Neural Science.

[47]   Kandel, Eric R.; James H. Schwartz, Thomas M. Jessell (2000). Principles of Neural Science.

If enough neurotransmitter is released and enough receptors are activated, the signal can continue its cycle to the brain or spinal cord. Examples of neurotransmitters include serotonin, adrenaline, and dopamine.[48]

Neurons differ in function and their location in the body. Sensory neurons are part of sensory organs. These organs and their neurons send their electrochemical signals via these nerves to the spinal cord and the brain. Motor neurons work the opposite way, and receive signals from the brain and spinal cord. These neurons cause muscle contractions and affect glands. Interneurons interconnect other neurons within the brain and spinal cord to act as in-between messengers.[49]

Sensory receptors are activated through their sensitivity to some physical modality, such as light or temperature. A primary nucleus (or multiple nuclei) located in the brain stem specifically gathers signals from these sensory receptor cells.[50]

A foremost purpose of the brain is to make sense of relevant information gathered from the sensory inputs and communicated via the body's neural network.[51] Beyond the classical five senses, our brains also process additional inputs, such as body temperature, balance, and composition of the bloodstream. Some animals, such as

---

[48]   Mouse Party. http://learn.genetics.utah.edu/content/addiction/drugs/mouse.html - This website features an online flash demonstration about how drugs effect the neurotransmitters in the brain. One specific worth noting is the mouse dedicated to Marijuana – as the chemical in THC is similar in structure to the chemical that removes unnecessary short term memories.

[49]   Rapport, Richard L. (2005) Nerve Endings: The Discovery of the Synapse. W. W. Norton & Company. pp. 1-37.

[50]   Kandel ER, Schwartz JH, Jessel TM. (2000). 4th ed. Principles of Neural Science. New York: McGraw-Hill Professional. Ch 21 and 30.

[51]   Kandel, ER; Schwartz JH, Jessel TM (2000). Principles of Neural Science.. Ch 21 and 30.

snakes, have additional senses including infrared heat sensors, or they use classical senses in non-traditional ways, such as the sonar of bats.[52]

Secondary areas that extract special information also exist. One compares the signals from the two eyes in order to create the effect of seeing a third dimension.[53] Each sensory system has a dedicated portion of the thalamus (the section of the brain that makes these comparisons) serves as a direct relay to the "primary" cortical area.

Additionally, a set of "higher-level" cortical sensory areas analyze the sensory input in specific ways. For the visual systems, there are areas that analyze color and identify objects.[54] There are other areas in the brain that combine the inputs from different sensory modalities. This part of the brain is best described as integrative rather than just sensory.[55]

3. ONE IF BY LAND... TWO IF BY SEA...

Before exploring the integrative purpose of the brain, it is necessary to understand the two types of messages that are sent to the brain from neurons that have received an impulse. One is chemical, the release of a neurotransmitter, while the other is electrical, the creation of an action potential.[56] This action potential dispenses with the "middleman" of the neurotransmitter and connects the two synaptic cells together by creating a voltage differential (an electrical charge) that can move quickly between cells.[57]

---

[52]   Kandel, ER; Schwartz JH, Jessel TM (2000). Principles of Neural Science.. Ch 21 and 30.

[53]   Kandel, ER; Schwartz JH, Jessel TM (2000). Principles of Neural Science.. Ch 21 and 30.

[54]   Ibid.

[55]   Ibid.

[56]   Schmidt-Nielsen K (1997). Animal Physiology: Adaptation and Environment (5th ed.). Cambridge: Cambridge University Press.

[57]   Zoidl G, Dermietzel R (2002). "On the search for the electrical synapse: a glimpse at the future". Cell Tissue Res. 310 (2): 137–42.

While neurotransmitters are effective for conveying information, electrical connections between synapses allow for faster transmission because they do not require diffusion over the space between the cells. Hence electrical synapses are used whenever a fast response and coordination of timing are relevant – such as the escape reflex, also known as the "fight-or-flight" response. The retinas in the eyes of vertebrates (animals with a backbone) contain electrical synaptic neurons also known as photoreceptors.[58]

Photoreceptors are capable of photo transduction, a process that converts electromagnetic radiation (light) into a change in the voltage of the cells membrane.[59] Until the 1990s, it was thought that there were only two types of photoreceptors: rods and cones. However, in 1991 Russell G. Foster and colleagues discovered a non-rod, non-cone photoreceptor in the eyes of mice, where it was shown to mediate the circadian rhythms more commonly known as the body's 24-hour biological clock.[60] These third photoreceptors respond much more sluggishly and signal the presence of light over the long term.[61] Their functional roles are unrelated to the formation of images and they differ fundamentally from those of pattern vision.[62] Instead they provide a stable representation of ambient light intensity.

These photoreceptors play a major role in synchronizing circadian rhythms to the 24-hour light/day cycle by sending electrical impulses directly into the circadian pacemaker of the brain, the hypothalamus.

---

[58]   Zoidl G, Dermietzel R (2002). "On the search for the electrical synapse: a glimpse at the future". Cell Tissue Res. 310 (2): 137–42.

[59]   Kandel, E. R.; Schwartz, J.H.; Jessell, T.M. (2000). Principles of Neural Science.

[60]   Foster RG, Provencio I, Hudson D, Fiske S, De Grip W, Menaker M. Circadian photoreception in the retinally degenerate mouse (rd/rd). J Comp Physiol [A]. 1991 Jul;169(1):39-50

[61]   Wong KY, et al. ; "Photoreceptor Adaptation in Intrinsically Photosensitive Retinal Ganglion Cells". Neuron 48: 1001–1010.

[62]   Pattern vision is the term relating to the vision of infants – vision focused on patterns and not about form.

This third type of cell also regulates pupil size and other behavioral responses to ambient lighting conditions. They also contribute to the regulation or suppression of the release of melatonin.[63]

It is for this third reason that the third type of photoreceptor is so important. Melatonin is known as the hormone of darkness. Contrary to initial belief, Melatonin production is inhibited by light and permitted by darkness,[64] specifically by blue light[65] at wavelengths of 484 nanometers. [66]Melatonin can positively alter electrophysiological processes associated with memory, such as the creation of long-term memories.[67] One of the many functions that melatonin performs is to promote sleepiness, and it is this role that is most relevant to this paper. In addition, extremely high doses of melatonin (50 mg) dramatically increased REM sleep and dream activity.[68] Furthermore, many psychoactive drugs, including marijuana and LSD, increase melatonin synthesis. It has even been suggested that certain types of hallucinogenic drugs emulate melatonin activity in the awakened state.[69]

---

[63]   Zaidi FH, et al. "Short-wavelength light sensitivity of circadian, pupillary, and visual awareness in humans lacking an outer retina." Curr Biol. 2007 Dec 18;17(24):2122-8

[64]   Brainard GC, Hanifin JP, Greeson JM, Byrne B, Glickman G, Gerner E, Rollag (August 15, 2001). "Action spectrum for melatonin regulation in humans: evidence for a novel circadian photoreceptor". J Neurosci. 15;21 (16): 6405–12.

[65]   Kayumov L, Casper RF, Hawa RJ, Perelman B Chung SA, Sokalsky S, Shipiro (May 2005). "Blocking low-wavelength light prevents nocturnal melatonin suppression with no adverse effect on performance during simulated shift work". J Clin Endocrinol Metab. 90 (5): 2755–61.

[66]   Roberts JE (2005). Update on the positive effects of light in humans. 490–2.

[67]   Larsen J et al (2006). "Impaired hippocampal long-term potentiation in melatonin MT2 receptor-deficient mice." Neurosci Lett **393** (1): 23–6.

[68]   Lewis, Alan (1999). Melatonin and the Biological Clock. McGraw-Hill. pp. 23.

[69]   Ibid.

Additionally, melatonin has been shown to prevent the formation of neurofibrillary tangles, which have been found in the hypothalamus of patients with Alzheimer's disease. These tangles adversely affect patient's abilities to form long-term memories.[70]

4. MELATONIN IS AN IMPORTANT INGREDIENT FOR SLEEP

Sleep is controlled by our circadian clocks and our willed behavior (within certain boundaries). The circadian clock is an inner timekeeping, temperature-fluctuating, enzyme-controlling device that works in tandem with adenosine, a neurotransmitter that inhibits many of the bodily processes associated with wakefulness.[71] Adenosine is created throughout the day – with high levels leading to sleepiness. Additionally, the release of melatonin and the gradual decrease in core body temperature lead to sleep.[72]

Adenosine is created over the course of the day; high levels of adenosine lead to sleepiness. In diurnal versus nocturnal animals, sleepiness occurs as the circadian element causes both the release of the hormone melatonin and a gradual decrease in core body temperature. The timing is affected by one's chronotype.[73] It is the circadian rhythm that determines the ideal timing of a correctly structured and restorative sleep episode.

---

[70] Wang X, Zhang J, Yu X, Han L, Zhou Z, Zhang Y, Wang J (2005). "Prevention of isoproterenol-induced tau hyperphosphorylation by melatonin in the rat". *Sheng Li Xue Bao* **57** (1): 7 – 12.

[71] Wyatt, James K.; Ritz-De Cecco, Angela; Czeisler, Charles A.; Dijk, Derk-Jan (01 October 1999). "Circadian temperature and melatonin rhythms, sleep, and neurobehavioral function in humans living on a 20-h day". Am J Physiol 277 (4): R1152–R1163.

[72] Wyatt, James K.; Ritz-De Cecco, Angela; Czeisler, Charles A.; Dijk, Derk-Jan (01 October 1999). "Circadian temperature and melatonin rhythms, sleep, and neurobehavioral function in humans living on a 20-h day". Am J Physiol 277 (4): R1152–R1163.

[73] *Chronotype* is an attribute of human beings reflecting whether they are alert and prefer to be active early or late in the day

There are two types of sleep in humans: Rapid Eye Movement (REM) and Non-Rapid Eye Movement (NREM) sleep. The American Academy of Sleep Medicine (AASM) further divides NREM into three stages: N1, N2, and N3, the last of which is also called delta, or slow-wave, sleep (SWS).[74] Healthy sleep must include the appropriate sequence and proportion of NREM and REM phases, as each plays a different role in the memory consolidation-optimization process.

During REM sleep, certain neurotransmitters are inhibited from being released, and as a result the motor neurons are not stimulated, resulting in a condition known as REM atonia. However, REM sleep does not prevent sensory neurons from firing.

Harvard sleep researchers Saper and Stickgold point out that an essential part of memory and learning consists of nerve cell dendrites' sending information to the cell body to be organized into new neuronal connections[75]. This process demands that no external information be presented to these dendrites, and they suggest that this may be why it is during sleep that we solidify memories and organize knowledge.[76]

5. REM SLEEP IS THE KEY TO MEMORY RENDERING

Jie Zhang proposed that dreaming is a result of brain activation and synthesis, and that dreaming is not directly connected to REM sleep, as they are controlled by different brain mechanisms.[77] Zhang hypothesized that REM sleep suspended the motor neurons thus freezing the body, while simultaneously processing, encoding and transferring the data from the temporary memory to the long term

---

[74]   Silber, et al. (2007). "The Visual Scoring of Sleep in Adults". J Clin Sleep Med (American Academy of Sleep Medicine) 3: 121–31

[75]   Why Sleep Matters. Harvard Medical School. Web.

[76]   Ibid.

[77]   Zhang, Jie (2005). Continual-activation theory of dreaming, Dynamical Psychology. Web.

memory. Unfortunately, there is not much evidence to support or disprove this theory.

Zhang makes the assumption that during REM sleep, the unconscious part of the brain is busy processing the procedural memory while the conscious part of the brain "disconnects" from the inputs of the sensory organs.[78] This triggers a "continual-activation" mechanism to generate a data stream that stores these memories in the conscious part of the brain. Zhang suggests that this pulse-like brain activation is the inducer of each dream. He proposes that because of the involvement of the brain's associative thinking system, dreaming is self-maintained within the dreamer's own thinking until the next pulse of memory causes new associations to form. This explains why dreams have both characteristics of continuity (within a dream) and sudden changes (between two dreams).[79]

Regardless of whether or not Zhang is correct, his theory makes sense when examined with a few other studies. Throughout the sleep and wakefulness continuum[80] the central nervous system synthesizes a conception of reality from externally gleaned information. When one is awake sensory input feeds current data, contextual and motivational information to the Central Nervous System. During sleep, sensory input is limited, with remnants of sensory data and earlier expectations constructing reality.[81] In the dream state, perception occurs without the constraints of external sensory input.[82]

---

[78]   Admittedly this disconnect is not a complete severance because there exists "dream incorporation," whereby an external stimulus (usually auditory) becomes a part of a dream eventually awakening the dreamer. A famous painting by Salvador Dalí depicts this concept. It is titled *Dream Caused by the Flight of a Bee around a Pomegranate a Second Before Awakening* (1944).

[79]   Zhang, Jie (2005). Continual-activation theory of dreaming, Dynamical Psychology. Web.

[80]   Wolf, F. A. (1995). The dreaming Universe. New York: Simon & Schuster.

[81]   LaBerge, Stephen. "Deaming and Consciousness".

[82]   Ibid.

In a study published in the journal Human Brain Mapping, participants who were in REM "dream" sleep were also monitored by special MRI imaging designed to visualize brain activity. The researchers found activity in areas of the brain that control sight, hearing, smell, touch, balance and body movement.[8384]

6. THESE STIMULI MANIFEST THEMSELVES AS SHORT TERM MEMORIES, LONG TERM MEMORIES, OR JUNK.

There are two types of memory, long term and short term (or working) memory. These memories are created by consolidation, which is the process of stabilizing a memory trace after the initial acquisition.[85]

Consolidation is differentiated into two specific processes, synaptic consolidation, which occurs within the first few hours after learning and system consolidation, where hippocampus-dependent memories become independent of the hippocampus over a period of weeks to years.[86] Recently a third process, called reconsolidation, has become the focus of research. When it takes place previously consolidated memories can be reopened for change again through reactivation of the memory trace.

Short-term memory is the brain's system for remembering information "in use." Most people can only hold five to nine items in their short-term memory at one time. If they try to remember more than that, they

---

[83]   Hong, Charles Chong-Hwa, et al. ""FMRI Evidence for Multisensory Recruitment Associated with Rapid Eye Movements during Sleep."

[84]   "Rapid Eye Movement (REM) Study Shows Brain Functions Same Way Awake Or Asleep." Newswise.com.

[85]   Dudai, Y. (2004). The neurobiology of consolidations, or, how stable is the engram? Annu. Rev. Psychol., 55, pp. 51-86

[86]   Dudai, Y. (2004). The neurobiology of consolidations, or, how stable is the engram? Annu. Rev. Psychol., 55, pp. 51-86

will often end up forgetting the "middle" items.[87] Eight uninterrupted seconds are required to encode an image into short-term memory. [88]

7. WHAT MAKES MEMORIES STICK?

Signals are transferred between cells via the synapse. The strength of the connection between the synapses (and the effectiveness of the system to convey the message and/or store the memory, changes depending upon the amount and type of stimulation passing through (chemical or electric). The strength of the connection can be short term – lasting seconds or minutes – or can last even longer.

In short-term memory, the brain's cerebral cortex receives chemical or electrical messages from the sensory neurons. The sensory stimulus can create a conversion from one type of signal (chemical or electrical) to the other type of signal. This conversion triggers alterations of synaptic proteins. These alterations affect the efficiency of the synapse for future connections. These changes generally last seconds to minutes.

Long-term repeated or continuous synaptic activation, known as long-term potentiation, results in the production of a second messenger molecule that initiates a permanent altering of the neuron's structure. Learning and memory have been linked to these permanent changes to the structure of neurons.

The process of rooting long-term memories may be disrupted by specific drugs, antibodies and gross physical trauma.[89] This is why victims of head trauma are unable to remember events leading up to the incident. The stimulation that went from the sensory cells to the other neurons will not be able to alter the protein structure of the neurons prior to the trauma.

---

[87]   "Nine Brain Quirks You Didn't Realize You Had". Web.

[88]   Luckily for the photographer, viewers generally examine the contents of a gallery presentation for more than eight seconds apiece

[89]   Dudai, Y. (2004). The neurobiology of consolidations, or, how stable is the engram? Annu. Rev. Psychol., 55, pp. 51-86

The proteins created from the changes in synaptic plasticity store "memories" on something akin to an electronic tape loop (although some scientists debate the existence of that loop). Once a complete loop is made, three things can happen: 1) the information can be 'rehearsed' (repeated) silently or aloud, which will provide auditory cues; 2) the information goes into long-term memory; or 3) the information will be lost.

John Mackin, scientist, conceives of working memory as composed of three functions: "the central executive (an attentional controlling system) and two slave systems: the visuo-spatial sketch pad, which manipulates visual images, and the phonological loop, which stores and rehearses speech-based information.[90]

In 1974 Baddeley and Hitch proposed a working memory model which replaced the concept of general short-term memory with specific, active components.[91] According to this model, working memory consists of three parts: the central executive, the phonological loop and the visuo-spatial sketchpad. In 2000 this model expanded to include the multimodal episodic buffer.[92]

The central executive is the "traffic light" that channels information to the other component processes. It is currently believed that while these processes act with a similar intention, they may actually consist of a group of individual processes working together.

The phonological or "articulatory loop" as a whole deals with sound or phonological information. It consists of two parts, a short-term phonological store with auditory memory traces that are subject to

---

[90]   Warren, Suzanne. "Memory and the Brain". Web.

[91]   Baddeley AD (2000). The episodic buffer: a new component of working memory? Trends in Cognitive Science, 4, 417-23.

[92]   Baddeley AD (2000). The episodic buffer: a new component of working memory? Trends in Cognitive Science, 4, 417-23.

rapid decay and an articulatory rehearsal component that can revive the memory traces.[93]

Any auditory verbal information is assumed to enter into the phonological store automatically. Information presented visually can be transformed into phonological code by silent articulation and then encoded. This transformation is facilitated by the articulatory control process. The phonological store acts as an inner ear, remembering speech sounds in their temporal order, while the articulatory process acts as an inner voice and repeats the series of words (or other speech elements) on a loop to prevent them from decaying.[94]

The visuospatial sketchpad is assumed to hold information about what we see. It is used in the temporary storage and manipulation of spatial and visual information, such as remembering shapes and colors, or the location or speed of objects in any particular plane. The sketchpad can be divided into separate visual, spatial and possibly kinesthetic (movement) components. It is principally represented within the right hemisphere of the brain.[95]

Logie has proposed that the visuospatial sketchpad can be further subdivided into two components: 1). The visual cache, which stores information about form and color and 2) the inner scribe, which deals with spatial and movement information. It also rehearses information in the visual cache and transfers information to the central executive.[96]

The episodic buffer is yet another subsystem dedicated to linking information across domains. It integrates units of visual, spatial, and

---

[93]   Baddeley AD (2000). The episodic buffer: a new component of working memory? Trends in Cognitive Science, 4, 417-23.

[94]   Ibid.

[95]   Baddeley AD (2000). The episodic buffer: a new component of working memory? Trends in Cognitive Science, 4, 417-23.

[96]   Baddeley AD (2000). The episodic buffer: a new component of working memory? Trends in Cognitive Science, 4, 417-23.

verbal information with time sequencing (or chronological ordering), such as the memory of a story or a movie scene. The episodic buffer is also assumed to have links to long-term memory and semantic meaning.[97]

Long-term memory is that part of our "memory storage system that has unlimited capacity to retain information over an extended time."[98] At least three different types of memory are included in long-term memory: procedural, declarative, and remote.

Procedural memory represents motor or skill learning without verbal mediation or encoding. Examples include walking or riding a bicycle. Such memories are slow to acquire but greatly resist change or loss. Hence it is said that once a person learns to ride a bicycle, she will never forget.

Declarative memory is for facts, such as names or dates. Such memories are quick to acquire and quick to lose. Declarative memory requires conscious recall, in that some conscious process must call back the information. Apparently this is by design, as it allows for our brains to pay attention to meaningful or relevant stimuli and ignore uninformative information.[99]

Declarative memory can be further subdivided into semantic and episodic memory. Semantic memory allows the encoding of abstract knowledge about the world, such as "Paris is the capital of France". These are facts that exist independent of context, whereas episodic memory concerns information specific to a particular context.. Episodic

---

[97]   Baddeley AD & Wilson B A(2002). Prose recall and amnesia: implications for the structure of working memory. Neuropsychologia, 40, 1737-1743.

[98]   Warren, Suzanne. "Memory and the Brain". Web.

[99]   "Short Term Memory and How to Sharpen the Mind." Web. Jan 2010.

memory is used for more personal memories, such as the sensations, emotions, and personal associations of a particular place or time. [100]

In contrast, procedural memory (or implicit memory) is not based on the conscious recall of information, but on implicit learning. Procedural memory is primarily employed in learning motor skills and should be considered a subset of implicit memory. When given a specific task, most people improve their performance with repeated practice. This is not the result of new explicit memories; rather individuals are accessing aspects of their previous experiences. [101]

Remote memories are foundation memories upon which more recent memories are built. Because these are obviously linked to many new memories, they are less subject to change or loss.

8. WHERE DO MEMORIES LIVE?

Both long- and short- term memories are composed of three processes: encoding, storage, and retrieval. [102] These processes occur in various locations in the brain. It is speculated that the hippocampus is involved in the creation of long-term memory, but recent evidence suggests that it acts more as a processor than a storage facility.

As Irving Kupferman explains, "[L]ong-term memories are stored in multiple regions throughout the nervous system. (In other words, they are not localized but stored through circuitry)". [103] Procedural memory involved in long-term motor learning depends on the cerebellum and basal ganglia. [104] Furthermore Kupferman also noted "reflexive and declarative memory formation may involve different circuits in the

---

[100]   Gleitman H. (1991) Psychology, 7, 275-278.

[101]   Ibid.

[102]   Warren, Suzanne. "Memory and the Brain". Web.

[103]   Warren, Suzanne. "Memory and the Brain". Web.

[104]   Gleitman H.(1991)Psychology, 7, 275-278.

brain. Reflexive memory relies on the cerebellum and amygdala; formative, on the hippocampus and temporal lobes."[105]

Does this mean that memory could live outside the body? Dr. Rupert Sheldrake suggests that memory does not reside in any geographic region of the brain, but instead in a kind of field surrounding and permeating the brain. Meanwhile, the brain itself acts as a "decoder" for the flux of information produced by the interaction of people with their environment.[106]

Sheldrake cites a report by Karl Lashley, a research neurophysicist who demonstrated that even after up to 50 percent of a rat's brain had been cut away, the rat could still remember the tricks it had been trained to perform.[107] It did not matter which side of the brain was removed. Most importantly it was not a phenomenon exclusive to rats.

The hippocampus is associated with episodic memories of personally experienced events and their associated emotions.[108] These are memories that relate stories. Damage to the hippocampus results in the inability to form new long-term episodic memories (though there is no effect on the encoding of procedural, or skill, memories).[109] Perhaps that is inherent to our design, as well; different brain areas devoted to personal survival and consciousness.

These permanent changes to neuron cells, resulting in what we have determined is long-term memory, can be induced either by strong stimulation of a single pathway to a synapse, or cooperatively via the

---

[105]   Warren, Suzanne. "Memory and the Brain". Web.

[106]   Vintiñi, Leonardo. "Epoch Times - Does Memory Reside Outside the Brain?" Epoch Times - National, World, China, Sports, Entertainment News. 29 Aug. 2008. Web. Jan. 2010.

[107]   Ibid.

[108]   Anissimov, Michael. "What Is the Hippocampus?" WiseGEEK: Clear Answers for Common Questions. Web. Jan. 2010.

[109]   Anissimov, Michael. "What Is the Hippocampus?" WiseGEEK: Clear Answers for Common Questions. Web. Jan. 2010.

weaker stimulation of many. [110] Therefore different types of stimuli, such as visual, olfactory or auditory, can trigger memories when each stimulus on its own would be too weak to do so.

9. HOW DO YOU MAXIMIZE STIMULATION?

By maximizing the type of stimulation that a particular photograph produces –the photographer increases the likelihood that such stimulation will trigger other memories stored within the human neural net.

Visual phototransduction (briefly mentioned earlier) is a process by which light is converted into electrical signals in the photosensitive cells of the retina of the eye. This conversion occurs by altering the charge of the photoreceptor's membrane. This in turn charges the bipolar cell, which then signals to the nervous system that light is in the visual field. [111]

When light hits a photoreceptive cell (which are located in the back of the retina), the pigment contained within changes shape. The pigment contains proteins called opsin, and different ratios of the type of opsin lead to different eye colors. [112], [113] The opsin is attached to an organic molecule called retinal (which is a derivative of vitamin A). The retinal changes its structure in the presence of light. This change causes a regulatory protein to be produced that causes changes to the synapses

---

[110]   McNaughton BL (April 2003). Long-term potentiation, cooperativity and Hebb's cell assemblies: a personal history. Philosophical transactions of the Royal Society of London. Series B, Biological sciences 358 (1432): 629–34.

[111]   Ibid.

[112]   McNaughton BL (April 2003). Long-term potentiation, cooperativity and Hebb's cell assemblies: a personal history.

[113]   Moiseyev G et al et al . (2005) RPE65 is the isomerohydrolase in the retinoid visual cycle. Proc. Nat. Acad. Sci.

causing it to have a negative charge. This is unlike any other sensory cell that would provide for a positive charge.[114]

The hyperpolarization of the cell stops the release of the neurotransmitter glutamate. Glutamate has the unique ability to depolarize some neurons while hyperpolarizing others, creating an antagonistic environment specifically with regards to bipolar cells.

There are two types of bipolar cells, on-center and off-center. An on-center cell is stimulated when the center of its receptive field is exposed to light, and is inhibited when the surrounding is exposed to light. Off-center cells have just the opposite reaction. On the edge between the two, in mammals, an on-off switching effect is present. [115]

In an "on-center" cell, stimulation of the center of the receptive field produces depolarization and an increase in the firing of the ganglion cell. Stimulation of the surrounding produces a hyperpolarization and a decrease in the firing of the cell. Stimulation to both – produces only a mild response. This prevents an overload of signals to the brain. The opposite is true for an "off-center" cell. This allows the cells to transmit contrast, and it is contrast that ultimately provides for the most stimulation.[116]

The center-surround organization of the cells allows them to transmit not only light exposure but also about the differences in firing rates between the center and surroundings. This is where we determine contrast. Discontinuities in the distribution of light falling on the retina specify the edges of objects.

---

[114]   Moiseyev G et al et al . (2005) RPE65 is the isomerohydrolase in the retinoid visual cycle. Proc. Nat. Acad. Sci.

[115]   Ibid.

[116]   Moiseyev G et al et al . (2005) RPE65 is the isomerohydrolase in the retinoid visual cycle. Proc. Nat. Acad. Sci.

By using high-contrast lighting in my portfolio I am able to optimize the effectiveness of the stimulation reflected from the surface of my photographs. The specific science of how I applied this is detailed later with a section on dynamic range. Additionally, this application is not limited to choice of camera equipment but also in final presentation/output.

The previous section explains the pathway that stimulus takes from the sensory cells to the brain. However, not all stimuli are created equal, therefore it is necessary to understand the unique nature of the sensory cells in order to maximize their receptiveness to stimulation.

There are three types of photoreceptive cells located on the retina. The two best understood are rods and cones. Cones are less sensitive than rods and are used primarily for daylight vision. Rods are used in low light conditions. Rods and cones are not evenly distributed across the retina; cones predominate the center while the rods prevail in the periphery. [117]

Humans optimally have three kinds of cones, each of which responds best over a particular wavelength. The three cones are referred to as long, middle, and short, though they can be called by their primary color recognition – red, green, blue. Each cone sends a binary signal (either on or off) to the retina, and color is determined by the ratio at which cells send the signal and at what frequency. [118]

10. ARE RODS AND CONES UNIVERSALLY EFFECTIVE? OR DO PEOPLE SEE THE WORLD DIFFERENTLY?

While having three kinds of cones is ideal, it is not always the case. The genes for the red and green cones are located on the X chromosome. Women have two X chromosomes, so they are twice as likely to have one fully functional copy of the gene. Males only have

---

[117]   Vision and Art: The Biology of Seeing, Margaret Livingstone, 25 (2002).

[118]   Ibid, 26/27 (2002).

one X-chromosome, and therefore are much more likely to possess a mutation that affects one of those two cones.

Ten percent of men (and less than one percent of women) are red/green color blind because of a mutation in the gene. Blue cone color blindness, the condition affecting John Dalton and myself, is much rarer as everyone has two copies of the blue cone gene.[119] The unusual individuals who do lack the blue color cone have trouble distinguishing some bluish colors from some yellows and greens.[120]

I suspect I am one of the few individuals that have a mutation of both my blue cone genes. Informal testing supports my hypothesis. For the sake of this paper, let us assume that my vision is blue impaired,. Therefore it would make sense that the color yellow would provide f the maximum amount of stimulation that my eyes could detect.

The optimum wavelength to stimulate the red cone is 650nm. The optimum wavelength to stimulate the green cone is 520nm. The optimum wavelength for the blue cone is 420nm.

[119]   Vision and Art: The Biology of Seeing, Margaret Livingstone, 34 (2002).

[120]   Ibid, 35 (2002).

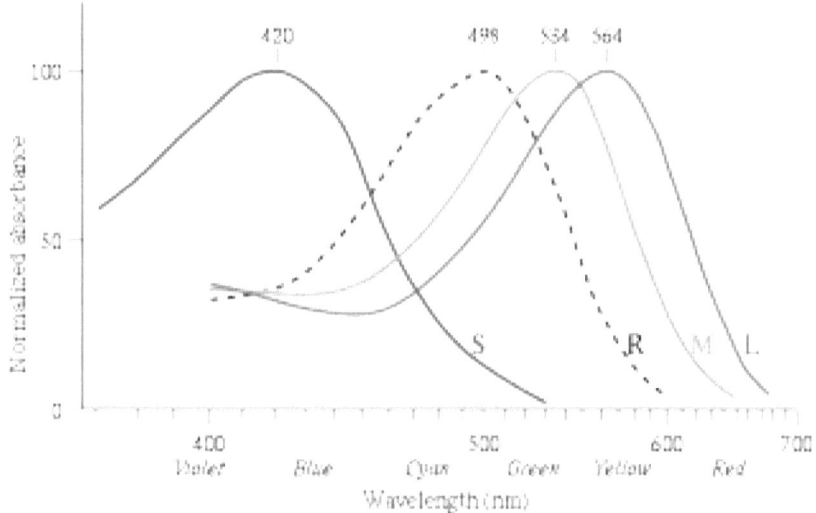

The average wavelength shared between the three is 498nm (a cyan/green). However, the stimulation of the blue cone at that frequency is minimal. The red and green cones are also stimulated at an amount less than optimum.

If we take the blue cone out of the equation, as is potentially the case with my own vision, the average frequency that would stimulate both of the remaining cones would be approximately 550nm. It produces a greenish-yellow hue. This light frequency is the optimum for stimulation in a two-coned system, and one of the few zones that optimally stimulate multiple cones in a three-coned system.

11. HOW DO I CAPTURE THIS YELLOW LIGHT? HOW DO EYES SEE AND HOW CAN I GET THAT IN A CAMERA?

On the most basic level our eyes look for the greatest areas of contrast among images. But there must be a distinction made among the scenes containing high-contrast ratios that causes us to focus on one rather than the other. In particular, humans prefer to look at images of faces. Daphne Maurer, psychology professor and researcher at McMaster University, studied babies just minutes after birth and found that they prefer looking at designs that resemble faces. And by just a few days old, a baby will look longer at their own mother's face than at those of strangers.[121]

Based upon the input from our sensory cells, our brains are able to identify the simple physical aspects of a person's face, which usually results in the ability to determine age, gender, or basic facial expressions. This initial information is used to create a structural model of the face, which allows it to be compared to other faces in memory even if viewed in differing perspectives. The structural model of the face is then transferred to what Maurer terms notational "face recognition units" that are used with "personal identity nodes" to identify a person through information stored in the semantic memory.[122]

Most scientists agree that during the perception of faces, major activations occur in the extrastriate areas of the brain bilaterally, particularly in the fusiform gyri and in the inferior temporal gyri.[123,124] The fusiform gyrus is part of the temporal lobe. Its full function is not yet known, but testing has already begun. Studies by Gauthier[125] have shown that the fusiform gyrus is active during facial recognition. Furthermore, it is also active when study participants were asked to discriminate between different types of birds and cars. Elaborating further, this part of the brain became active when participants become experts at distinguishing between computer generated nonsense shapes

[121]   Pitman, Teresa. "Can Babies Recognize Faces?" Today's Parent Magazine | Parenting Resource, Advice, Help, Tips & Articles for Canadian Parents. Nov. 2004. Web. Jan. 2010.

[122]   Andreasen N. & et al. (1996). "Neural substrates of facial recognition". J Neuropsychiatry Clin Neurosci 8 (2): 139–46. Web. Jan. 2010.

[123]   Kanwisher N et al (01 June 1997). "The fusiform face area: a module in human extrastriate cortex specialized for face perception". *J. Neurosci.* **17** (11): 4302–11. Web. Jan. 2010.

[124]   Andreasen N. & et al. (1996). "Neural substrates of facial recognition". J Neuropsychiatry Clin Neurosci 8 (2): 139–46.

[125]   Gauthier, et al(February 2000).Expertise for cars and birds recruits brain areas involved in face recognition. *N*at. Neurosci. **3** (2): 191–7.

known as greebles.[126] It is generally concluded that this part of the brain is responsible for the processing of color information, face and body recognition, word and number recognition, and within-category identification.[127]

At least one study has captured the FFA in action. A 2009 magnetoencephalography study found that objects incidentally perceived as faces, an example of pareidolia[128] evoke an early (165 ms) activation in the FFA, at a time and location similar to that evoked by faces, whereas other common objects do not evoke such activations. This activation is similar to a slightly earlier peak at 130 ms seen for images of real faces. The authors suggest that face perception evoked by face-like objects is a relatively early process, and not a late cognitive reinterpretation phenomenon.

A recent study by Pawan Sinha, an associate professor of brain and cognitive sciences at MIT, concluded that a key factor for facial recognition involved the ratio between a person's eyes (darker) and their forehead and cheeks. The test involved identifying faces from photo negatives, and Sinha theorized that photo negatives are hard to recognize because they disrupt these very strong regularities around the eyes.[129] Furthermore, there is evidence suggesting that autistic patients

---

[126]   The Greebles refers to a category of novel objects used as stimuli in psychological studies of object and face recognition, created by Scott Yu at Yale University. They were named by the psychologist Robert Abelson. The greebles were created so as to share constraints with faces: they have a small number of parts in a common configuration. This makes it difficult to distinguish any individual object on the basis of the presence of a feature, and this is thought to encourage the use of all features and the relationships between them. In other words, greebles, like faces, can be processed configurally.

[127]   McCarthy G et al. (1997) Face-specific processing in the human fusiform gyrus.J. Cognitive Neuroscicence. 9, 605-610.

[128]   Pareidolia is a psychological phenomenon involving a vague and random stimulus (often an image or sound) being perceived as significant.

[129]"   MIT: Why We Have Difficulty Recognizing Faces in Photo Negatives | E! Science News." E! Science News | Latest Science News Articles. 18 Mar. 2009. Web. Jan. 2010.

tend to focus on the mouths of people rather than their eyes. The contrast ratio of other parts of the face, such as the mouth, are not nearly as consistent, making facial identification much more difficult.[130]

This leads me to conclude that high contrast images that show the eyes of the subject darker than the rest of the subject's face are much easier to recognize and relate to. This largely results from the super-stimulation of the Reticular Activating System, a section of the upper brainstem that includes the FFA.

The RAS is a monitoring and switching clearinghouse in which both internal and external stimuli pass. They integrate the regulation of cardiovascular, respiratory and motor response to external stimuli. RAS cells receive information via adjacent connections from neurons located in ascending sensory neural tracts and relay that information directly to higher cerebral structures. Integration of the cerebral cortex and the RAS enables us to be aware and knowledgeable about activities in our environment.

B. APPLYING THE CONCEPT OF CONTRAST TO THE IMAGES

Emily's face is obscured in most of the images. This was deliberate in order to stimulate the parts of the brain related to trying to identify faces. By recognizing that a face exists within the frame, the viewer's brain is bombarded with stimuli in the appropriate regions. Difficulty in identifying the face further activates the regions of the brain responsible for facial identification, thereby maximizing the brain's release of the additional chemical and electronic stimulation.

---

[130]   MIT: Why We Have Difficulty Recognizing Faces in Photo Negatives | E! Science News." E! Science News | Latest Science News Articles. 18 Mar. 2009. Web. Jan. 2010.

Physically, Emily was ideally suited to be the subject for this body of work. Her pale complexion with her darker eyes and occasional glasses help reinforce the high-contrast present in most faces.

C. WE MUST BE OPEN TO RECEIVING THESE BRAIN MESSAGES

Of course, this super stimulation is useless if we are not capable of responding to stimuli. The human mind must be conscious, meaning it s aware and responsive to stimuli. The brain must be highly aroused, which occurs in both awake and sleep cycles. The level of brain arousal, measured by electrical or metabolic brain activity, fluctuates according to circadian rhythms and is influenced by lack of sleep, drugs and alcohol, physical exertion, etc. in a predictable manner.

Given the previous scientific analysis, I hypothesize that by deactivating all of the visuals, an otherwise normal individual would experience would significantly reduce the dimensionality of their conscious experience as no color, shape, motion, texture, or depth could be perceived.

Arousal increases when we are exposed to something that has personal meaning, – such as seeing a familiar face, hearing music, viewing a photograph, experiencing a type of light, etc.[131] Yet when the body experiences REM sleep – a state completely devoid of motor activity and external stimulation– the body also experiences heightened arousal. . During this phase, the metabolic and electrical activity is similar to those during conscious and vivid states.

This lends even more weight to the mounting evidence that our dreams and our reality contain similar stimuli. The key difference is that our perceived reality is fueled by physical stimulation, while our subconscious and our dreams are fueled by previously experienced or imagined stimulation.

---

[131]   Baars BJ (1993) A cognitive theory of consciousness. New York: Cambridge University Press.

1. The Camera as Camera

The camera is the means by which a photographer captures his selected aspects of reality. There exist an endless plethora of collection devices, but if the purpose is to accurately simulate the human sensory experience, the viable options are significantly fewer. I have selected three Leica cameras, each with a specific paired lens as optimal capture devices. In my opinion, they all exhibit similar qualities and share distortions (or lack thereof) with the human eye.

Every photograph has a fundamental flaw preventing it from being an accurate depiction of a captured reality, and that is its inherent misrepresentation of dimensionality. While a photo may appear to have three dimensions, there is no actual third dimension beyond the medium in which the photograph is printed. This is a deliberate but inaccurate condition resulting from the use of a single lens during capture. Accuracy is not entirely related to believability, as our higher mental functioning inherently allows us to look beyond flaws, including the misconstruction of time from viewing a captured instant indefinitely in order to interpret the reality captured.

To create believability in a photograph it is necessary to use a camera and lens that have similar qualities to that of the human eye. Lenses are measured by means of their focal length and their aperture. The focal length of an optical system is a measure of how strongly it converges (focuses) or diverges (defocuses) light. For an optical system in air, it is the distance over which initially collimated rays are brought to a focus.

A lens with a focal length approximately equal to the diagonal size of the film or sensor format is known as a normal lens; its angle of view is similar to the angle subtended by a sufficiently large print viewed at a typical viewing distance of the print diagonal, which therefore yields a normal perspective when viewing the print.[132] If the frame size is

---

[132] LD. Stroebel. (1999). View Camera Technique. Focal Press. p. 135–138.

24mm x 36mm, the diagonal is 43.267mm.[133] If the frame size is 30x45mm, the diagonal is 54.083mm.[134]

Most manufacturers market the 50mm lens (actually a few mm larger) as the normal lens, because it is the optimum focal length with zero distortion. The problem is that a 50mm lens only affords a 46-degree field of view that is significantly less than the human field of vision, which is closer to a 24mm lens. However, if we were to use such a wide-angle lens, our images would suffer significant distortion that does not appear when using a normal lens. Our brains have the ability to compensate for this distortion, however the camera does not. Therefore the 50mm lens is considered to be optimal, because of its lack of distortion.

There are two factors inherent to any lens; the focal length and the amount of light passing through, known as its aperture or f-number. As with any lens, computing the f-number of the human eye involves measuring the physical aperture and the focal length. In tests the human pupil can be as large as 6-7mm wide open, which translates into the maximum physical aperture. However, the entrance pupil is typically about 4 mm in diameter, although it can range from 2 mm (f/ 8.3) in a brightly lit place to 8 mm (f/ 2.1) in the dark.[135,136]

Also intrinsic to any lens is the ratio between the size (and shape) of the aperture to the out-of-focus areas contained within an image. A photographer may choose a lens that renders out-of-focus points of light in ways that are pleasing to the eye. A photographer's choice to highlight portions of a photograph by means of prominent out of focus regions is an example of selective form providing cues for narrative content.

---

[133]   Muralidhar, Ajoy. "Does a 50mm Normal Lens Really See What the Eye Sees?" *Olympus/Zuiko*. 5 Sept. 2007. Web. Jan. 2010.

[134]   This calculation refers to the Leica S2, which has a frame size larger than 35mm film.

[135]   Hecht E. (1987). Optics (2nd ed.). Addison Wesley. Sect. 5.7.1

[136]   Robinson, Linda. Art of Professional Photography (2007). Web.

There are many 50mm lenses that are f/2.1 or faster. The race for the optimum [137] optic started in Japan in 1953 with the introduction of the Zunow 1.1/50mm lens, followed in 1954 with the Fujinon 1.2/50mm, but has since ended with the recent release of the Leica .95 Noctilux.

These original lenses, namely the Zunow and the Fujinon lenses, were offered in both Canon and Leica screw thread mounts. Comparably, the 1.1 and 1.2 presented a significant difference from a previous standard of 1.5. Canon and Nikon responded in 1956 with a 1.2/50mm lens with seven elements (canon) and a 1.1/50mm lens with nine elements (Nikon). Though Nikon and Canon were focusing on SLR development, Canon did introduce the .95/50mm lens for the Canon 7 in 1961.

Canon then introduced a 1.2/58mm lens that utilized aspherical surfaces in 1971. The first series used aspherical surfaces that were ground by manually operated machines. Only later (but long before Leica) did Canon switch to a fully automatic grinding process.

An aspheric lens or asphere is a lens whose surfaces have a profile that is neither a portion of a sphere nor of a circular cylinder. The asphere's more complex surface profile can reduce or eliminate spherical aberration and also reduce other optical aberrations, as compared to a simple lens.[138] A single aspheric lens can often replace a much more complex multi-lens system. The resulting device is smaller and lighter, and possibly cheaper than the multi-lens design. Aspheric elements are used in the design of multi-element wide-angle and fast normal lenses to reduce aberrations.

According to Canon's original advertisement for the .95 lens, it "holds razor sharpness even at full aperture." In fact the Canon lens set at maximum aperture is an excellent practical example of the working of spherical aberration. Spherical aberration is an optical effect in lenses

---

[137]   Optimal for the purpose of representing the human perspective believably.

[138]   Meister, Darryl. "Ophthalmic Lens Design." OptiCampus.com - Online Optical Continuing Education. Web. Sept. 2009.

that occurs due to the increased refraction of light rays when they strike a lens or a reflection of light rays when they strike a mirror near its edge, in comparison with those that strike nearer the center. It signifies a deviation of the device from the norm, and results in an imperfection of the produced image.

Spherical aberration should not be confused with barrel distortion; whereas barrel distortion affects the shape of the image, spherical aberration affects its sharpness.

A high-speed lens with optimum optical sharpness is the desired pinnacle for any camera system. The marketing argument has focused on the use in low ambient or natural light or even the absence of illumination where the just hand-holdable shutter speed could be the dividing line between a good and a lost picture.

Almost every design of optimum optical lenses relied on spherical lens surfaces. The designer needed additional lens elements and more exotic properties and/or daring shapes to get a decent quality at the widest apertures. The pictures that could be made with these lenses could be described as acceptable only with a sympathetic approach. Canon was overzealous in producing its 0.95/50mm lens for its rangefinder camera, having lost sight of the ideal in usability in favor of having achieved the benchmark of speed.

Around 1965, several manufacturers abandoned the rangefinder format, leaving Leitz as the sole survivor. Leitz took this opportunity to produce a lens to rival the Canon .95 lens, the last viable lens of that type on the market.

Their research into the design options indicated that the only solution for a lens that combined a compact mount with high performance was to use aspherical surfaces. The aperture of the original Noctilux was set to f/1.2. A wider aperture required a bigger mount and it is possible that the size of the lens elements was too large for the aspherical grinding process.

The successor of the original Noctilux widened the maximum aperture to f/1.0 and used only spherical surfaces. The performance wide open was better than what the Canon .95 offered, perhaps because of the new glass types available to the Leica designers.

The Noctilux 1.0/50mm stayed in production from 1976 until 2008, when a new version was produced. The designers opted for the 0.95 aperture, with an 11 percent increase in pupil diameter, which provided significant need for chromatic correction. The new Noctilux 0.95 has a more rigorous correction of aberrations over the entire field. Wide open, the differences are less pronounced than with the previous version, but are still interesting enough to analyze. The design of the lens is state of the art with a floating element, aspherical surfaces and a selection of new glass types specifically selected for this design.

Wide open the lens shows a certain softness of major subject outlines. The lower contrast of the high frequencies and fine textural details softens the edges of the low frequencies or outlines of major subject shapes. Stopping down to 1.2 does improve the overall contrast, even more so at 1.4, although contrast is also modified in post processing.

At an aperture of 0.95, it should be clear that this lens outperforms the human eye in terms of allowing more light to expose the frame than the human counterpart. However, the Noctilux is special for two other reasons beyond its speed. The first is its freedom from flare. Even with light shining almost directly into the lens, flare is minimal. Considering the conditions for usage of such a lens, this is a remarkable quality.

Secondly, it showcases an extremely narrow depth of field when shooting wide open. Depth of field is measured in inches, as opposed to feet, and consequently the background will be even more out of focus. The Noctilux, by design, renders out of focus areas very smoothly, lending an almost impressionistic quality to those areas.

This impressionistic quality allows the artist to compose the elements of the photograph to be featured in this manner. The gaze of the viewer will then tend to linger over these points of interest. Elements are arranged with consideration of several factors (known variously as the principles of organization, principles of art, or principles of design) into a harmonious whole that works together to produce the desired statement, a phenomenon commonly referred to as unity.

One of the defining features of the impressionist statement is a quality of fuzziness from diffused light. To obtain this characteristic in images, artists must balance spherical aberration to manipulate out-of-focus points of light, called bokeh. The word "bokeh" comes from the Japanese word "boke" (pronounced bo-keh) which literally means fuzziness or dizziness. It is the aesthetic quality of the blur, "the way the lens renders out-of-focus points of light."[139]

Pleasing bokeh doesn't happen automatically in lens design. Perfect lenses render out-of-focus points of light as circles with sharp edges, but ideal bokeh would render each of these points as blurs, not hard-edged circles. Good bokeh prefers a Gaussian distribution.

A technically perfect lens has no spherical aberration. Therefore a perfect lens focuses all points of light as cones of light behind the lens. The image is in focus if the film is exactly where the cone reaches its finest point, which shrinks as lens quality improves.

If the film is not exactly where that cone of light reaches its smallest point, then that point of the image is not in focus. Then that point is rendered on film as a disk of light, instead of as a point. This disc is also called the "blur circle," or "circle of confusion" by people calculating depth-of-field charts. In a lens with no spherical aberration, this blur circle is an evenly illuminated disc. Out-of-focus points all look like perfect discs with sharp edges. This is not optimal for bokeh, because the sharp edge of these discs begins to give definition to things intended to be out-of-focus.

---

[139]   Ono, Philbert. "PhotoGuide Japan-PhotoWords-Lens." PhotoGuide Japan. 5 Apr. 2007. Web. Dec. 2009.

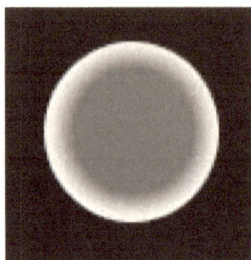

Fig. 1. Poor Bokeh. This is a greatly magnified blur circle showing very poor bokeh. A blur circle is how an out-of-focus point of light is rendered. Note how the edge is sharply defined and evenly emphasized for a point that is supposed to be outoffocus, and that the center is dim.

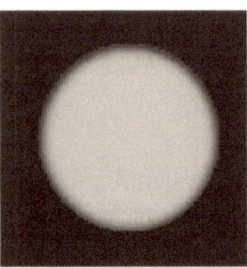

Fig 2. Neutral Bokeh. This is a technically perfect and evenly illuminated blur circle. This does not promote bokeh either, because the edge is still well defined. Out-of-focus objects, either points of light or lines, can effectively create reasonably sharp lines in the image due to the edges of the sharp blur circle. This is the blur circle from most modern lenses designed to be "perfect."

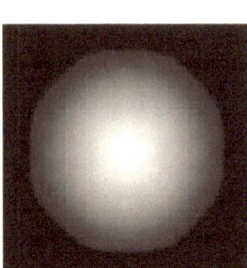

Fig. 3. Good Bokeh. Here is what we want. This is great for bokeh since the edge is completely undefined. This also is the result of the same spherical aberration, but in the opposite direction, of the poor example seen in Fig. 1. This is where art and engineering start to diverge, since the better-looking image is the result of an imperfection. Perfect bokeh demands a Gaussian blur circle distribution, and lenses are designed for the neutral example shown in 2.) above.

There are no perfect lenses, so one usually does not see these perfect discs. Furthermore, spherical aberration means that the discs made by out-of-focus points on the subject will not be evenly illuminated. Instead they tend to have more of the light collect in the middle of the disc or toward the edges. Here are some illustrations:

The position of the viewer can strongly influence the aesthetics of an image, even if the subject is entirely imaginary and viewed "within the mind's eye." By exerting creative control over the bokeh, a photographer can create or reduce depth to influence the viewer's interpretation of the subject.

A subject can be rendered more dramatically when it fills the frame. There exists a tendency to perceive things as larger than they actually are, and filling the frame fulfills this psychological mechanism. Bokeh can be used to eliminate distractions from the background.

Bokeh is often most visible around small background highlights, such as specular reflections and light sources, which is why it often associated with such areas. However, bokeh is not limited to highlights, as blur occurs in all out-of-focus regions of the image.

2. THE CAMERA SYSTEM

There were three distinct cameras used during the course of this project. The initial images taken for this project were done so in 35mm film using a Leica M7 Titanium camera. I used Fuji Superia 1600 iso color film and had the film processed and the negatives scanned by my lab. I had been shooting with the latest edition of the 1.0/50mm Noctilux.

Shortly after shooting a few times in film, I acquired the Leica M9. I began shooting with the latest 1.0/50mm Noctilux, but later acquired the newer 0.95 Noctilux and shot exclusively with that thereafter, both in film and digital formats.

The last camera was the Leica S2 equipped with the 70mm 2.5 lens. The S-series lenses have been referred to being the most amazing lenses that Leica – a master crafter of lenses – had ever made.[140] It was questionable as to whether or not this could be achieved given the need for the lens to cover the extra surface area of the larger chip.

---

[140]   Harrison, Matthew B. "Additional Thoughts and Images – Leica S2." *The Leica Guy*. 6 Jan. 2010. Web. Jan. 2010.

The bokeh is quite pleasing. It's not the Noctilux. Either version. But it's certainly something noticeably pretty. It is also consistently sharp with minimal to no distortion from edge to edge.[141]

I chose Leica cameras for this demanding project because the optics are superior to all except for the human eye; the equipment is portable and reliable (despite the weather conditions); and scientifically, they were the best to create the necessary elements in order to super stimulate the viewers' senses.

D. APPLYING THE THEORY OF CONTRAST

My portfolio features images with higher-than-average contrast. I have always adopted this as a personal style, but the science of how the sensory cells process light signals explains why I tend to favor this aesthetic in my work; higher contrast images produce higher electrical stimulation in the neural net.

Contrast is the range between the lightest part of a scene and the darkest part. In photography this range is called Dynamic Range, and it is the range of luminance values of a scene being photographed. When used to describe any particular equipment, dynamic range usually refers to the limits of the luminance range that a given camera or film can capture.[142]

Our visual reality contains scenes with near infinite dynamic range. A major limiting factor of this near infinite dynamic range is the human eye. Despite this, the human eye is an amazing tool. The human visual system has a dynamic range in excess of 13 f/stops. The dynamic range of digital sensors generally is less than that of the human eye and almost certainly is not as wide as that of chemical photographic media. However, digital chips manufactured for Leica cameras have the same

---

[141]   Harrison, Matthew B. "Additional Thoughts and Images – Leica S2." *The Leica Guy*. 6 Jan. 2010. Web. Jan. 2010.

[142]   Myszkowski K et al, (2008). High Dynamic Range Video. Morgan & Claypool Publishers.

or better dynamic range than all of the best dSLR cameras, regardless of manufacturer.[143] The Leica M9, the film used in the Leica M7, and the Leica S2 all have dynamic ranges near 11 stops.

However, algorithms have been developed allowing images to be mapped differently in the shadows and highlights in order better distribute light across the entire image. This is known as HDR (High Dynamic Imaging) and was not incorporated into this project.

My person philosophy is that while the possibilities using HDR are seemingly endless, the limitations imposed by the output and processing mediums (the prints, and the computers/screens) prevent anyone from truly enjoying the full range of what they had created. Until the output technology evolves, in my opinion, it is not a tool whose future is certain, as without a tangible manifestation, any expectation of permanence is ludicrous.

By using equipment that captures the broadest dynamic range, I maximize the contrast present in the final image, making the photographs more appealing to the viewer. The only remaining limitation on this range is the output medium.

1. BRUSHED ALUMINUM PRINTS

Because my primary focus was to maximize contrast within the images, the exclusive use of Leica equipment was outstanding in achieving this goal. However as I began developing the images, I realized the print medium was compromising the final contrast levels in the final output. Under average conditions with average materials, the dynamic range of paper colored by ink is 6 f/stops. So the use of average materials under average conditions lost any additional dynamic range afforded by the Leica cameras.

---

[143]   This is based upon my personal analysis of the individual reports created by DxO labs; a company devoted to studying things such as the dynamic range of camera sensors and the amount of distortion in lenses.

At the recommendation of my advisor, I explored output options involving a higher dynamic range material , such as brushed aluminum. I settled on a dye sublimation process normally reserved for commercial applications that could be applied for my fine art needs.

Dye sublimation is a simple enough concept. Special dyes are printed onto a transfer paper by means of a patent-pending process and then infused into a patented coating using pressure and heat. Metal prints have an archival value rivaling the best giclées or photographic processes. [144]

Additionally, these prints have a waterproof and ultra-hard coating that is virtually scratch proof. The archival value of a print should be judged not only by its resistance to degradation by ultraviolet light and ozone exposure, but also to moisture and surface damage. When these additional factors are incorporated into the equation, these metal prints are without a doubt, the best way to preserve an image.

Preservation is a major theme running throughout this thesis process. It would only make sense to output these images to a medium that can withstand the test of time, especially considering that the location did not. As evidenced by the images contained within this portfolio, the metal skeleton is really the only part of the abandoned greenhouse still standing. It wasn't the paper, cloth, or glass elements that remained. [145]

Lastly, the reason they are glossy –is so that you can see yourself in them. [146]

---

[144]   Rochester Institute of Technology is currently running accelerated aging tests on metal prints. Preliminary results should be available soon.

[145]   These are staple output mediums for photographs.

[146]   Insert "rimshot" here.

2. THE ASPECT RATIO 2:3.

35mm film was originally used for movies. The aspect ratio for movies during the sound era was 1.37. This ratio was nearly universally used in movies between 1932 and 1953. The usage was so widespread that it was adopted as the official ratio in 1932 by the Academy of Motion Picture Arts and Sciences.

Two major sociological shifts occurred in the early 1950s that changed this. The first was television's saturation into more than 50 percent of American homes, and then as a result, movie studios introducing a widescreen format.[147]

Because the standard for cinema presentations was 35mm film, and all of the movie houses had projectors that only functioned with that size film, the movie industry   had to create a widescreen effect with the same size film. Two popular techniques for doing so resulted in the wasting of area within the visible frame either before recording or during presentation[148] in order to create the widescreen effect. It wasn't until 1954, with the invention of Super 35, that filmmakers were able to maximize their usage of the film without wasting the available image information.

The film frame was cropped with standard 35mm to allow for the necessary room to house the soundtrack. The Super 35 frame size is 24.89mm x 18.66mm, compared to the standard for Academy 35mm film of 21.95mm x 16.00mm, the new frame size provides 32% more image area than the standard format.

The concept is the same for cinema as it is in photography. As it stands now, still photography's usage of the 35mm film is equally a waste of data collecting real estate. Though the film is 35mm wide, only 24mm

---

[147]   Forner, Jeffrey. "Aspect Ratio FAQ." *Home Theater Forum*. Web. Jan. 2010.

[148]   Forner, Jeffrey. "Aspect Ratio FAQ." *Home Theater Forum*. Web. Jan. 2010.

of those 35mm are usable because 11mm are needed to properly transport the film through the camera. It was determined at the time of Thomas Edison's original motion picture camera invention that the other dimension should be 36mm as that is twice the size of a single movie frame.

This sets the aspect ratio of the first Leica camera at 2:3. This is an aspect ratio that has continued in the new high-end digital products. Considering this has been an established format for most of the 20th century, there is a subconscious identification with visual images of that aspect ratio and their printing. Additionally, this relationship to film comes with the cache of an association of veracity. Viewers were primed to believe 35 mm images were truth because the early use of film photography (especially Leica) was photojournalism.

CONCLUSION

These photographs convey a personally constructed story about myself as performed by model, muse, and fiancée, Emily Therese. They were created to convey stimulation to the mind of the viewer in order to trigger a memory. In my situation, the memory is my own involving the creation of these photographs and our exploration at the abandoned greenhouse.

These photographs are also a metaphor for my own personal emotional growth from dealing with the death of my mother and an obsession with abandoned medical facilities into re-appropriating my resources into creating this new life for myself.

These photographs also were constructed in such a way as to maximize the stimulation of the sensory cells in the mind of other viewers. The intent is to trigger additional or nearby memories from within the human neural net, thereby connecting the viewer with the photograph by means of a much more meaningful personal relationship than with other photography.

Bibliography

Andreasen, NC, DS O'Leary, S. Arndt, T. Cizadlo, R. Hurtig, K. Rezai, GL
Watkins, LB Ponto, and RD Hichwa. "Neural Substrates of Facial
Recognition." *The Journal of Neuropsychiatry & Clinical
Neurosciences* 8 (1996): 139-46. Web. Jan. 2010.
<http://neuro.psychiatryonline.org/cgi/content/abstract/8/2/139>.

Anissimov, Michael. "What Is the Hippocampus?" *WiseGEEK: Clear Answers
for Common Questions*. Web. Jan. 2010.
<http://www.wisegeek.com/what-is-the-hippocampus.htm>.

Arbib, Michael A. *The Handbook of Brain Theory and Neural Networks*.
Cambridge, Mass.: MIT, 2003. Print.

Baars, Bernard J. *A Cognitive Theory of Consciousness*. Cambridge:
Cambridge UP, 1993. Print.

Baddelay, A. D. "Prose Recall and Amnesia: Implications for the Structure of
Working Memory." *Neuropsychologia* 40 (2002): 1737-743.
ScienceDirect. Web. Jan. 2010.
<http://www.sciencedirect.com/science?_ob=ArticleURL&_udi=B6T
0D-45PJY96-
2&_user=10&_coverDate=12%2F31%2F2002&_rdoc=1&_fmt=high
&_orig=search&_sort=d&_docanchor=&view=c&_searchStrId=1311
665383&_rerunOrigin=google&_acct=C000050221&_version=1&_u
rlVersion=0&_userid=10&md5=052d2e7aca479467d40784071b7b11

74>.

Baddelay, A. D. "The Episodic Buffer: a New Component of Working

Memory?" *Trends in Cognitive Science* 4 (2000): 417-23. Web. Jan.

2010.

<www.nbu.bg/cogs/events/2002/materials/Markus/ep_bufer.pdf>.

"The Brain-addiction Connection : Neurons and Neurotransmitters | All About

Addiction." *All About Addiction - Addiction Help and Advice.* 3 June

2009. Web. 12 Dec. 2009. <http://www.allaboutaddiction.com/the-

brain-addiction-connection-neurons-and-neurotransmitters/>.

Brainard, George C., John P. Hanifin, Jeffrey M. Greeson, Brenda Byrne,

Gena Glickman, Edward Gerner, and Mark D. Rollag. "Action

Spectrum for Melatonin Regulation in Humans: Evidence for a Novel

Circadian Photoreceptor." *The Journal of Neuroscience* 21.16 (2001):

6405-412. *Action Spectrum for Melatonin Regulation in Humans:*

Evidence for a Novel Circadian Photoreceptor. The Journal of

Neuroscience, 2001. Web. Jan. 2010.

<http://www.jneurosci.org/cgi/content/full/21/16/6405>.

Davies, Melissa. "Neuroscience - A Journey Through the Brain." *University of*

Alberta - Edmonton, Alberta, Canada. University of Alberta, 10 Apr.

2002. Web. 1 Jan. 2010.

<http://www.ualberta.ca/~neuro/OnlineIntro/Index.htm>.

Dudai, Y. "The Neurobiology of Consolidations, Or, How Stable Is the

Engram?" *Annual Review of Psychology* 55 (2004): 51-86. Print.

Forner, Jeffrey. "Aspect Ratio FAQ." *Home Theater Forum*. Web. Jan. 2010.
    <http://events.hometheaterforum.com/home/wsfaq.html>.

Foster, R.G., I. Provencio, D. Hudson, S. Fiske, W. De Grip, and M. Menaker.
    "Circadian Photoreception in the Retinally Degenerate Mouse
    (rd/rd)." *Journal of Comparative Physiology A: Neuroethology,
    Sensory, Neural, and Behavioral Physiology* 169.1 (1991): 39-50.
    SpringerLink. Web. 10 Dec. 2010.
    <http://www.springerlink.com/content/h56l45848637r35h/>.

Gauthier, Isabel, Pawel Skudlarski, John C. Gore, and Adam W. Anderson.
    "Expertise for Cars and Birds Recruits Brain Areas Involved in Face
    Recognition." *Neuroscience* 3.2 (2000): 191-97. Nature America, Inc.
    Web. Jan. 2010.
    <http://cognitrn.psych.indiana.edu/rgoldsto/courses/concepts/gauthier
    2000.pdf; http://neurosci.nature.com.>.

Gleitman, Henry, James J. Gross, and Daniel Reisberg. *Psychology*. 7th ed.
    New York: W. W. Norton & Company. Print.

Harrison, Matthew B. "Additional Thoughts and Images ? Leica S2." *The
    Leica Guy*. 6 Jan. 2010. Web. Jan. 2010.
    <http://www.theleicaguy.com/2010/01/06/additional-thoughts-and-
    images-leica-s2/>.

Hecht, Eugene, and Alfred Zaja?c. *Optics*. Reading, Mass.: Addison-Wesley

Pub., 1987. Print.

"History Overview." *BTI Boyce Thompson Institute for Plant Research.* Web.

1 Jan. 2010. <http://bti.cornell.edu/history.php>.

Hong, Charles Chong-Hwa, James C. Harris, Godfrey D. Pearlson, Jin-Suh

Kim, Vince D. Calhoun, James H. Fallon, Xavier Golay, Joseph S.

Gillen, Daniel J. Simmonds, Peter C. M. Van Zijl, David S. Zee, and

James J. Pekar. "FMRI Evidence for Multisensory Recruitment

Associated with Rapid Eye Movements during Sleep." *Human Brain

Mapping* 30.5 (2008): 1705-722. *FMRI Evidence for Multisensory

Recruitment Associated with Rapid Eye Movements during Sleep.*

InterScience, 28 Oct. 2008. Web. Jan. 2010.

<http://www3.interscience.wiley.com/journal/121494129/abstract?C

RETRY=1&SRETRY=0>.

Kandel, Eric R., James H. Schwartz, and Thomas M. Jessell. *Principles of

Neural Science.* 4th ed. New York: McGraw-Hill, Health Professions

Division, 2000. Print.

Kanwisher, Nancy, Josh McDermott, and Marvin M. Chun. "The Fusiform

Face Area: A Module in Human Extrastriate Cortex Specialized for

Face Perception." *The Journal of Neuroscience* 17.11 (1997): 4302-

311. Yale University. Web. Jan. 2010.

<camplab.psych.yale.edu/articles/Kanwisher_97JN.pdf>.

Kayumov, Leonid, Robert F. Casper, Raed J. Hawa, Boris Perelman, Sharon

66

A. Chung, Steven Sokalsky, and Colin M. Shapiro. "Blocking Low-Wavelength Light Prevents Nocturnal Melatonin Suppression with No Adverse Effect on Performance during Simulated Shift Work." *Journal of Clinical Endocrinology & Metabolism* 90.5 (2005): 2755-761. *Blocking Low-Wavelength Light Prevents Nocturnal Melatonin Suppression with No Adverse Effect on Performance during Simulated Shift Work*. Journal of Clinical Endocrinology & Metabolism. Web. Jan. 2010. <http://jcem.endojournals.org/cgi/content/full/90/5/2755>.

LaBerge, Stephen. "Dreaming and Consciousness." Speech. Toward a Science of Consciousness Conference. Tucson, AZ. Jan. 2010. *Dreaming and Consciousness*. 9 Apr. 1996. Web. <http://www.lucidity.com/Tucson2.abs.html>.

Larsen, J., RE Jessen, T. Uz, M. Kurtuncu, M. Imbesi, and H. Manev. "Impaired Hippocampal Long-term Potentiation in Melatonin MT2 Receptor-deficient Mice." *Neuroscience Letters* 393.1 (2006): 23-26. Print.

Lewis, Alan E., and Dallas Clouatre. *Melatonin and the Biological Clock: the Amazing Hormone That Combats Aging and Renews Health*. New Canaan, Conn.: Keats Pub., 1996. Print.

Livingstone, Margaret. "Do You See Red Like I See Red?" *Vision and Art: the Biology of Seeing*. New York: Abrams, 2008. 33. Print.

McCarthy, Gregory. "Face-Specific Processing in the Human Fusiform Gyrus." *Journal of Cognitive Neuroscience* 9.5 (1997): 605-10. Print.

McNaughton, Bruce L. "Long-Term Potentiation, Cooperativity and Hebb's Cell Assemblies: A Personal History." *Philosophical Transactions: Biological Sciences* 358.1432 (2003): 629-34. *JSTOR.* Web. Jan. 2010. <http://www.jstor.org/pss/3558161>.

Meister, Darryl. "Ophthalmic Lens Design." *OptiCampus.com - Online Optical Continuing Education.* Web. Sept. 2009. <http://www.opticampus.com/cecourse.php?url=lens_design/&OPTI CAMP=f1e4252df70c63961503c46d0c8d8b60#asphericity.>.

"MIT: Why We Have Difficulty Recognizing Faces in Photo Negatives | E! Science News." *E! Science News | Latest Science News Articles.* 18 Mar. 2009. Web. Jan. 2010. <http://esciencenews.com/articles/2009/03/18/mit.why.we.have.diffic ulty.recognizing.faces.photo.negatives>.

Moiseyev, Gennadiy, Ying Chen, Yusuke Takahashi, Bill X. Wu, and Jian-Xing Ma. "RPE65 Is the Isomerohydrolase in the Retinoid Visual Cycle." *National Academy of Sciences. RPE65 Is the Isomerohydrolase in the Retinoid Visual Cycle.* 22 Aug. 2005. Web. Jan. 2010. <http://www.pnas.org/content/102/35/12413.full>.

"Mouse Party." *Learn.Genetics?.* The University of Utah. Web. 3 Feb. 2010. <http://learn.genetics.utah.edu/content/addiction/drugs/mouse.html>.

Muralidhar, Ajoy. "Does a 50mm Normal Lens Really See What the Eye Sees?" *Olympus/Zuiko*. 5 Sept. 2007. Web. Jan. 2010. <http://olympuszuiko.wordpress.com/2007/09/05/does-a-50mm-normal-lens-really-see-what-the-eye-sees/>.

Myszkowski, K., Rafa? Mantiuk, and Grzegorz Krawczyk. *High Dynamic Range Video*. [San Rafael, Calif.]: Morgan & Claypool, 2008. Print.

"Nine Brain Quirks You Didn?t Realize You Had - Stepcase Lifehack." *Stepcase Lifehack : Productivity, Getting Things Done and Lifehacks Blog*. 11 July 2007. Web. Jan. 2010. <http://www.lifehack.org/articles/productivity/nine-brain-quirks-you-didnt-realize-you-had.html>.

Ono, Philbert. "PhotoGuide Japan-PhotoWords-Lens." *PhotoGuide Japan*. 5 Apr. 2007. Web. Dec. 2009. <http://photojpn.org/words/len.html>.

Pitman, Teresa. "Can Babies Recognize Faces?" *Today's Parent Magazine | Parenting Resource, Advice, Help, Tips & Articles for Canadian Parents*. Nov. 2004. Web. Jan. 2010. <http://www.todaysparent.com/baby/article.jsp?content=20041007_1 04900_6020&page=1>.

"Rapid Eye Movement (REM) Study Shows Brain Functions Same Way Awake Or Asleep." *Newswise.com*. Newswise.com. Web. Jan. 2010. <http://newswise.com/articles/view/545801/>.

Rapport, Richard L. *Nerve Endings: the Discovery of the Synapse*. New York:

W.W. Norton, 2005. 1-37. Print.

Roberts, Joan E. *Update on the Positive Effects of Light in Humans*. Fordham University. Web. Jan. 2010. <http://faculty.fordham.edu/jroberts/Joan.pdf>.

Robinson, Linda. *Art of Professional Photography*. 1st ed. 2007. *L.Robinson-Art Professional Photography*. 11 Apr. 2009. Web. Nov. 2009. <http://www.scribd.com/doc/14156575/LRobinson-Art-Professional-Photography-2007>.

Schmidt-Nielsen, Knut. *Animal Physiology: Adaptation and Environment*. 5th ed. Cambridge [England: Cambridge UP, 1997. Print.

"Short Term Memory and How to Sharpen the Mind." *Sharpen Memory: Short-term Memory and How to Sharpen the Mind as Self Improvement*. Web. Jan. 2010. <http://www.learningandmemory.info/>.

Silber, Michael H., Sonia Ancoli-Isreal, Michael H. Bonnet, Sudhansu Chokroverty, Madeleine M. Grigg-Damberger, Max Hirshkowitz, Sheldon Kapen, Sharon A. Keenan, Meir H. Kryger, Thomas Penzel, Mark R. Pressman, and Conrad Iber. "The Visual Scoring of Sleep in Adults." *Journal of Clinical Sleep Medicine* 3.2 (2007): 121-31. *American Academy of Sleep Medicine*. American Academy of Sleep Medicine. Web. Jan. 2010. <http://www.aasmnet.org/jcsm/Articles/030203.pdf.>.

Stroebel, Leslie D. *View Camera Technique*. Boston: Focal, 1999. Print.

Vintiñi, Leonardo. "Epoch Times - Does Memory Reside Outside the Brain?"
  Epoch Times - National, World, China, Sports, Entertainment News.
  29 Aug. 2008. Web. Jan. 2010.
  <http://www.theepochtimes.com/n2/science-technology/sheldrake-
  morphogenic-field-memory-lashley-collective-unconscious-
  3486.html>.

Warren, Suzanne. "Memory and the Brain." Thesis. Bryn Mawr, 1997.
  Serendip's Exchange. Bryn Mawr, 18 Feb. 2002. Web. Jan. 2010.
  <http://serendip.brynmawr.edu/biology/b103/f97/projects97/Warren.
  html>.

"Why Sleep Matters." *Healthy Sleep*. Divison of Sleep Medicine at Harvard
  Medical School; WGBH Educational Foundation. Web. Jan. 2010.
  <http://healthysleep.med.harvard.edu/healthy/matters>.

Wolf, Fred Alan. *The Dreaming Universe: a Mind-expanding Journey into the
  Realm Where Psyche and Physics Meet*. New York: Simon &
  Schuster, 1995. Print.

Wong, Kwoon Y., Felice A. Dunn, and David M. Berson. "Photoreceptor
  Adaptation in Intrinsically Photosensitive Retinal Ganglion Cells."
  Neuron 48.6 (2005): 1001-010. *Electronic On-Site Archive*. CUNY
  Baruch College. Web. 31 Jan. 2010.

Wyatt, James K., Angela Ritz-De Cecco, Charles A. Czeisler, and Derk-Jan

Dijk. "Circadian Temperature and Melatonin Rhythms, Sleep, and Neurobehavioral Function in Humans Living on a 20-h Day." *American Journal of Physiology* 277.4 (1999): 1152-163. *AJP-Regulatory, Integrative, and Comparative Physiology*. American Journal of Physiology. Web. Jan. 2010. <http://ajpregu.physiology.org/cgi/content/full/277/4/R1152>.

Zaidi, F. H., J. T. Hull, S. N. Pierson, K. Wulff, D. Aeschbach, JJ Gooley, GC Brainard, K. Gregory-Evans, JF 3rd Rizzo, CA Czeisler, RG Foster, MJ Moseley, and SW Lockley. "Short-wavelength Light Sensitivity of Circadian, Pupillary, and Visual Awareness in Humans Lacking an Outer Retina." *Current Biology* 24.17 (2007): 2122-128. *ScienceDirect*. Web. 5 Feb. 2010. <http://www.sciencedirect.com/science?_ob=ArticleURL&_udi=B6VRT-4RBM5BB-1&_user=10&_coverDate=12%2F18%2F2007&_rdoc=1&_fmt=high&_orig=search&_sort=d&_docanchor=&view=c&_searchStrId=1311558471&_rerunOrigin=google&_acct=C000050221&_version=1&_urlVersion=0&_userid=10&md5=00e528607007520e14a09d1d71a4ee8e>.

Zhang, Jie. "Continual-activation Theory of Dreaming." *Dynamical Psychology* (2005). *Continual-activation Theory of Dreaming*. Dynamical Psychology. Web. Jan. 2010. <http://www.goertzel.org/dynapsyc/2005/ZhangDreams.htm>.

Zoidl, Georg. "On the Search for the Electrical Synapse: A Glimpse at the

    Future." *Cell and Tissue Research* 310.2 (2002): 137-42.

    Springerlink. Web. 12 Feb. 2010.

    <http://www.springerlink.com/content/due9fpmxdlg64wu1/>.

www.ingramcontent.com/pod-product-compliance
Lightning Source LLC
Chambersburg PA
CBHW030916180526

45163CB00004B/1862